D0208015

Teaching
LARGE
CLASSES
in
Higher Education

Teaching
LARGE
CLASSES

in

Higher Education

How to Maintain Quality
with Reduced Resources

EDITED BY

Graham Gibbs and Alan Jenkins

KOGAN
PAGE

First published in 1992

Kogan Page Limited
120 Pentonville Road
London N1 9JN

British Library Cataloguing in Publication Data

A CIP record for this book is available from the British Library.

ISBN 0 7494 0600 3

Typeset by Witwell Limited, Southport
Printed and bound in Great Britain by Biddles Ltd., Guildford and Kings Lynn

Contents

IMPROVING TEACHING AND LEARNING IN LARGE CLASSES

Notes on contributors

Graham Gibbs is the Head of the Oxford Centre for Staff Development at Oxford Polytechnic. He has led large national research and development programmes concerned both with quality and with large classes, including *Improving the Quality of Student Learning*, for the Council for National Academic Awards, and *Teaching More Students*, for the Polytechnics & Colleges Funding Council. He is the author of many practical books on teaching and learning, including five titles in the *Teaching More Students* series.

Alan Jenkins is a Principal Lecturer in Geography at Oxford Polytechnic and now works in its Educational Methods Unit. He has long taught the large introductory geography course in Year One, and has been a teaching assistant and instructor in large classes in American state universities. He is co-author of *Teaching Geography in Higher Education* (1991) and Chair of the Centre for Geography in Higher Education.

Harinder Bahra is a Senior Lecturer in Organisation Behaviour and Human Resource Management at Birmingham Polytechnic Business School, where he lectures on a mixture of undergraduate and postgraduate courses. His interests lie in developing individuals and organisations through organisation development and process intervention.

Clive Booth was appointed Director of Oxford Polytechnic in 1985. He was previously a senior officer of the Department of Education and Science and Her Majesty's Inspectorate, and was Deputy Director of Plymouth Polytechnic from 1981–84. A Cambridge educated biochemist, he took a PhD in Education Finance, as a Harkness Fellow, at the University of California Berkeley, in the early 1970s.

John Gold is a Senior Lecturer in Geography, and Joint Head of the Centre for Geography in Higher Education, at Oxford Polytechnic. He teaches courses in human geography and urban studies. He is co-author of *Teaching Geography in Higher Education* (1991) and currently editor of *Research into Higher Education Abstracts* and on the editorial boards of a number of higher education journals.

Ashley Green is a Senior Lecturer in Physics at Oxford Polytechnic, where he teaches courses in introductory physics, optics and astronomy. He is involved in the UK computers in Teaching Initiative (CTI) Physics Centre at the University of Surrey and in The Open University's Flexible Learning Approach to Physics (FLAP) project.

Martin Haigh is a Principal Lecturer and Field Chair in Geography at Oxford Polytechnic, where he teaches courses in soil conservation, physical geography and environmental philosophy. He also runs Oxford Polytechnic's Blaenavon Field Station, which is a complex of field experiments aimed at improving the quality of lands reclaimed from coal-mine spoils.

Julie Hartley is a Senior Lecturer in Organisation Behaviour at Birmingham Polytechnic. Her main interest is in programmes for part-time and mature students. She is the Course Director for the BA Business Studies part-time degree at Birmingham Polytechnic.

Ken Howells is Deputy Head of the School of Biological and Molecular Sciences at Oxford Polytechnic. He would like to find more ways to lessen the passive nature of science higher education.

Nick Johnson is a half-time Principal Lecturer in the Law Unit at Oxford Polytechnic. He is also Director of Education at Brecher & Company, a London firm of solicitors, where he is responsible for training and skills development.

Sue Piggott worked for many years as a Senior Lecturer in Pharmacology at Oxford Polytechnic before being seconded to Oxfordshire County Council, to develop a county-wide science ACCESS scheme. She is now Head of the Polytechnic's Continuing Education Centre, which plays an active part in Continuing Professional Development and other areas of adult education.

Andrew Ward, a former Oxford Polytechnic careers counsellor has worked as a researcher in industry and education. He is now a freelance writer.

David Watson has been Director of Brighton Polytechnic since September 1990. He was previously Principal Lecturer in Humanities at Crewe & Alsager College; Dean of the Modular Course; and Deputy Director at Oxford Polytechnic. His publications include *Managing the Modular Course* (1989), and *Developing Professional Education* (with Hazel Bines, 1992). Professor Watson has contributed widely to developments in the public sector of higher education, notably on the design and implementation of modular degree courses, and as a member of the Council for National Academic Awards and the Polytechnics and Colleges Funding Council.

Frank Webster is Chair of the Sociology Subject Committee at Oxford Polytechnic, where he teaches introductory and advanced courses in the discipline. He is author of *The New Photography* (1980), and co-author of *Information Technology: A Luddite Analysis* (1986) and *The Technical Fix: Education, Computers and Industry* (1989).

Chapter 1

An introduction: the context of changes in class size

Graham Gibbs and Alan Jenkins

SUMMARY

Since the early 1960s class sizes in British higher education have rapidly increased and are now approaching what is common in mass education systems elsewhere. However, the methods of delivering courses and the assumptions underpinning these methods have not significantly changed.

Many fear that this increase in student numbers without related increases in numbers of staff will result in a decline in quality. After reviewing the research evidence on class size and quality we argue that without rapidly changing teaching and assessment methods there will be a dramatic decline in the quality of British higher education. Though radical changes in teaching methods do not guarantee holding on to quality, they do offer the possibility of maintaining or slowing down the decline in quality and achieving an effective mass higher education system.

After outlining the case studies of innovations described in subsequent chapters it is argued that this British experience is relevant to all mass education systems that are attempting to improve the quality of undergraduate education.

The focus is on classes in which the possibility of individual relationships between professor and student is precluded, in which not every student who wants to speak in class can be called on, and in which grading essay exams can take up every evening and weekend of the course.

Maryellen Weimer (1987), *Teaching Large Classes Well*, p.2

We stack 'em deep and teach 'em cheap.

Utah Education Association Tee-Shirt

This book seeks to give practical assistance to those responsible for teaching large classes. It is initially addressed to those teachers and administrators in higher education in the UK who because of government pressures to teach more students at lower unit costs, find themselves teaching larger lectures, seminars, laboratories . . . than their experience as a student or teacher has prepared them for. We also consider that the suggestions for good practice contained here have relevance for teachers in those countries long accustomed to large classes.

Internationally, large classes are not a new phenomenon in higher education. In France, Holland or Italy first-year classes are commonly between 300 and 1,000 and sometimes very much larger. In North America, and particularly in the USA, large classes are the norm for much undergraduate work. Students in these countries wouldn't expect to see much of their professors on a personal basis until towards the end of their undergraduate careers, or even until their postgraduate work. Universities and Technical Institutes have developed ways of coping with such large numbers. These methods have their costs, particularly in terms of drop-out and failure, but people have got used to the methods used. It is almost taken for granted that courses operate in these ways. In marked contrast in the UK, classes have traditionally been very much smaller and contact between students and their tutors has been at the heart of the educational process. This has been comparatively expensive but as a result drop-out and failure have been very much lower. It is widely assumed (certainly by British academics) that the academic level students achieve, and the quality of work produced, is higher than in undergraduate courses in North America, and courses are generally shorter than in North America and the rest of Europe.

UK government policy and class size

Until recently UK higher education had certain central characteristics:

- Student entry was very selective, the assumption being that only the few could benefit from higher education.
- There was a strong emphasis on the teacher knowing the individual student so as to bring out the best of them academically.
- Written work, especially the essay, formed a principal way by which students were expected to both learn and be assessed.
- Class sizes were small.

The Robbins Report of 1963 (*Report of the Committee on Higher Education*, (1963) 105, Appendix 2a) which recommended an expansion of higher education, reported the following average number of students in a class:

	Lecture	Discussion Group	Practical
University	27.6	4.1	8.8
Technical College	14.2	8.4	7.9

The Hale Report similarly showed small class sizes were the norm, eg 'The median size of a lecture audience is 19 . . . (and that) few universities favour a seminar group greater than 12 and several put the maximum as low as 10' (*Report of the Committee on University Teaching Methods*, (UGC, 1964) 57, 62).

In the 1970s and 1980s, Labour and Conservative administrations sought to expand higher education at lower unit costs. The Thatcherite Conservative governments since 1979 have radically changed the spending mechanisms to force institutions to admit more students without relatedly increasing the number of staff. Thus staff–student ratios (SSRs) have decreased and class sizes have risen. Mergers of institutions (often accompanied by staff redundancies) have been part of this process of rationalisation.

One way these changes can be monitored is through the changes in staff–student ratios. Put simply, this is a ratio of full-time equivalent staff to full-time equivalent students. Government bodies and the institutions themselves have used staff–student ratios to allocate resources to institutions and particular disciplines. The universities have operated at more favourable staff–student ratios than polytechnics and colleges of higher education on the grounds that their greater commitment to postgraduate students and research necessitates more favourable funding. Similarly, a discipline such as physics, with its more intensive laboratory teaching, has operated at more favourable staff–student ratios than say art history (note that sometimes the term student–staff ratios is used).

In the 1980s expansion of student numbers occurred throughout British higher education, but the rate of expansion was greater in polytechnics and colleges than in universities. The expansion in student numbers was not uniform – governments and institutions tried selectively to expand certain subjects such as business studies and hold back or even cut others. Semi-enforced staff redundancies and limited and selective new appointments made for significant changes in staff–student ratios.

An Association of University Teachers (1990, 13–14) report, significantly entitled 'Goodwill Under Stress; Morale in UK Universities', reported that in the period 1970/71 to 1988/89 there was a 'steep rise in student–staff ratios' from 8.5:1 to 11.5:1.

Her Majestys Inspectors report that in the polytechnics and colleges of higher education ratios are worse: 'There are few institutions in which humanities and social science courses are taught with a staff–student ratio of less than 1:15 and many operate at ratios of nearer 1:20 or higher' (DES., 1991, 6). Such less favourable ratios reflect the lower funding per student received by these subjects and institutions. They also reflect the fact that in the 1980s expansion has been much faster in the polytechnics and college sector than in the university sector.

It is reasonable to assume that such pressures will accelerate. Academics who have experienced the last two decades as a period of rapidly worsening staff–student ratios, are faced with the nigh certainty of that increase significantly accelerating and the main increase immediately occurring in the universities. In 1991, a government paper on planned changes to higher education indicated further changes in funding mechanisms which would further pressure institutions to lower costs per students. In the House of Commons, Kenneth Clarke, the Secretary of State for Education stated:

Our policies are designed to ensure that higher education continues to expand efficiently alongside improvements in quality. When we came into office [ie 1979] only one in eight of the relevant age group went into higher education. Now it is one in five. *By the end of this decade, we expect one in three of all young people to benefit from higher education of our traditional high quality.* [Our emphasis]

House of Commons, 20 May 1991.

Though the opposition parties attacked aspects of these proposals the basic principle of large scale expansion of higher education at lower unit costs was endorsed. In short, the British higher education system is moving to an American style mass higher education system, where one of the central characteristics will be much larger class sizes. In those circumstances, can quality be maintained?

Does class size matter?

Does class size affect the quality of education? Quality itself is an elusive concept though it is now central to much of the public discussion of British higher education. Here we only want to sketch in some of the issues surrounding this term. Do we have some absolute conception of a relatively fixed quality, eg of what is a first class degree? Or will we accept the idea from some commercial and industrial worlds that quality is tied to function and we then talk about 'fitness for purpose'? In which case, our concern might be more with what society needs of someone with a first class degree or even whether we need many students with a first class degree. Do we mean the 'value added' as a result of a degree programme? If so what is 'value' – does it mean the grades received at the end of the course or what the student makes of the course (perhaps as an employee or as a citizen) much later? Do we focus on what trained observers tell us of what they observe of the process of education and/or do we listen to what those involved, particularly students and teachers, tell us of their views of the quality of their experience? To what extent are our conceptions of quality rooted in the values and assumptions of particular cultures and a particular time?

If quality is an elusive concept so is hard evidence as to the impact of class size on the quality of education. Though this issue has been extensively researched most of this research has been conducted at primary and secondary school level and has often involved small scale rigorously controlled studies. A meta analysis of many such studies concluded that there was: 'a substantial relationship between class size and teacher and pupil attitudes . . . [and that] smaller classes are associated with greater attempts to individualise instruction and better classroom climate' (Smith and Glass, 1980, 419). However, if one considers the effect of class size on student performance in formal tests a different picture emerges: 'Over the range of class sizes commonly found in schools (over the range of about 25–50 pupils) and for the kind of learning conducted in school classrooms, class size appears to play only a very minor role in determining eventual pupil performance on tests and examinations' (Andresen, 1991, 50).

Far fewer research studies have investigated the impact of size of class at college level. McKeachie (1986) summarising a number of studies done up until circa 1960 concluded that smaller classes were associated with critical thinking and were more popular with students. Feldman (1984) carried out a comprehensive study of the impact of class size and college students' evaluation of their teachers. He concluded that as class size increases, ratings of the course and the instructor declined slightly, and ratings of interactions and relationships between teachers and students declined dramatically. To be critical most of these college level studies don't take us very far in understanding the impact of size or what policy conclusions to draw from them.

One study that managed to isolate clearly the impact of class size at college level was that by Lindsay and Paton-Saltzberg (1987). This is a study that is doubly important to this book, for it manages to isolate the impact of size of class. Additionally, the study was on the students on Oxford Polytechnic's modular course, the setting for most of the case studies in this book. An extensive database concerning courses and students enabled Lindsay and Paton-Saltzberg to examine a variety of hypotheses. They considered the period 1981/2–1984/5, during which: 'student–staff ratios have increased, money allocated to individual students has been decreased in real terms and there has been a slight shift in student numbers towards technological subjects' (ibid, 213). Their central hypothesis was that: 'modules [a module is a course which represents about a twelfth of a full time student's work in an academic year] with larger numbers of enrolled students will have lower average marks than those with smaller numbers of students' (ibid, 216). As this was a period where enrolment on many courses was increasing, should their hypothesis be proven it would be a clear indication of the negative impact of increased class size on 'quality'.

Their results apparently confirmed this hypothesis:

The percentage of A and B+ grades awarded decreases steadily as module enrolment increases. There is a corresponding steady increase in B and C grades. Frequency of F grades appears to be constant and independent of enrolment. The absolute magnitude of these effects is surprising. The probability of a student gaining an A grade is less than half in a module containing 50–60 of what it is on a module enrolling less than 20 students (ibid, 217–8).

Evidently this is but one study; clearly though, it does suggest that if one's concern for quality centres in part on some students producing high quality work increased class size had negative impacts. Moreover, this was during the early years of deteriorating staff–student ratios; average class sizes at Oxford Polytechnic and elsewhere in the UK have risen significantly since this study (see Chapter Two).

Our job as staff developers takes us into many classrooms and discussions with teachers in a wide variety of disciplines and in many institutions. Drawing on what we have observed and what we have been told by teachers and students we assert that as class size increases so the practical problems faced by teachers and students become more marked, and change in nature. Whether it be in lecture, seminar, laboratory, or in the learning outside the classroom the experience of teachers and students changes with class size. These impacts of class size are described in Chapter Two and systematically considered in Chapter Three, Table 3.1.

We do not have a rigid interpretation of how many students make a class large. What is being taught and what resources, accommodation and facilities are available all have to be taken into account. We have seen teachers struggling to meet the needs of 40 students in a design studio which has work spaces for 18. Students who once had their own permanent workspace now share it with others. Even though class size is only 40, the experience of higher education is totally transformed for both teacher and students. We know of tutorial groups which have increased from six to ten and can no longer fit into staff offices for tutorials but now meet in laboratories or other unsuitable accommodation. We know of lectures which functioned satisfactorily with 60 present but which break down with 200. We know of institutions where students who wish to discuss their studies informally can find nowhere to sit on the college campus.

In addition, it is not just that the numbers enrolled on courses are increasing, it is also the case that the range of abilities and background in a class are becoming more varied. So the effects of increased class size and student numbers are complex and contextual.

But what is certain is that many staff experience it as a major problem and one which they see as severely affecting their ability to teach effectively. As we have seen, college teachers in the UK have been used to seminar classes of say 5–15 students, laboratory classes of about 10–20 and lectures from approximately 20–50. Now they are having to try to cope with classes up to 500 and it is likely that the rate of increase of student numbers and class size will accelerate. This is also occurring at a time when they are under much greater pressure to carry out and publish research and undertake consultancy.

A threat to quality?

Many fear that this has led to deterioration in the quality of British higher education and that further government pressures will accelerate that decline. The University Vice Chancellors argued to the government that: 'there was an overall decline in the quality of the student experience . . .' and that to enable expansion 'universities must be able to recruit more staff and reward them adequately' (*Times Higher Educational Supplement*, 17 May, 1991).

Diana Warwick, the general secretary of the Association of University Teachers, commenting on worsening staff–student ratios stated: 'University staff are teaching more students, classes are larger and *unless staff numbers are increased proportionally the quality of the UK degree will suffer'* (emphasis added). The size of classes was only one factor. Laboratory work, seminars and tutorials were all highly sensitive to the amount of time staff were able to devote to individual students: 'It is one of the most singularly envied characteristics of British higher education that students who need individual attention can get it. *Our reputation must suffer with every increase of student–staff ratios'* (emphasis added).

Perhaps these judgements – and those of the Secretary of State claiming 'traditional high quality' are tainted by self interest. However Her Majesty's Inspectors (HMIs) who systematically observe the quality of teaching and learning in polytechnics and colleges of higher education and give independent advice to government are beginning to comment publicly as to the dangers to quality posed by this expansion. A recent report on humanities and social science teaching commented:

A lot of effort . . . over the last ten years has gone into course and curriculum development. Relatively little attention has been paid to the methods of teaching and learning, which with some exceptions, are the same now as they have been for several decades. *The steady increase in the size of student groups has implications for methods of teaching and learning which have yet to be addressed in a systematic way . . . In many institutions . . . tutors continue to organise teaching and learning in ways which are no longer compatible with the numbers of students involved. In some cases this is beginning to have an adverse effect on the quality of work* [our emphasis].

(DES, 1991, 21, 7.)

Value judgements

Our own experience at the many institutions in the UK where we run workshops on teaching methods accords with the above judgement by HMIs. Many staff appear to be teaching and assessing in ways compatible with high staff–student ratios, low course enrolments, a highly selected student group and relatively high levels of laboratory and library resources per student.

We would question the effectiveness of much of this teaching and suggest that this pattern often worked because it could be oiled by easy and frequent individual exchanges between teacher and student. Ineffective lectures could be compensated for by brief explanations. Even though seminars were often dominated by the teacher and one or two students the rest were academically able enough to survive. When libraries were well stocked alternative sources of reading could be suggested or alternative essay topics negotiated. Students could be encouraged where student motivation had been ignored in course design, and guided where courses were vague as to their content and purpose. However one of the most prominent experiences of both students and lecturers in the new large classes has been that such informal exchange has all but disappeared. Many staff find their time and energy being stretched to breaking point and feel that they are no longer reaching the professional standards they wish to attain. The traditional pattern has broken down, its inherent weaknesses now exposed. The weaknesses are now so extensive and so prominent that the pretence is no longer sustainable. (Some of the evidence for these value judgements is reported in Chapter Two.)

We believe it is possible for British higher education to expand significantly in student numbers without a proportionate increase in teaching staff, for more of the student and staff experience to be in larger courses and still to hold on to something that most of us could recognise as quality if and only if:

1. individuals, departments, institutions and the system at large are willing radically to reappraise methods of teaching, learning and assessment; and
2. there is an honest reappraisal of what will be lost and gained in the process. The traditional pattern of frequent and intensive interaction between teachers and students on a one-to-one basis has already been lost and cannot be regained. Politicians who deny the validity of lecturers' concerns by glib statements about traditional high quality do not contribute to this honesty. Nor do academics' beliefs that more staff and more pay for them will somehow bring back a golden age.

When we have made similar statements in our institution or elsewhere, some – including many whose judgements we respect – have attacked us for aiding institutional rationalisation and threatening academic quality. We recognise that at times we run that risk. However we also assert:

- The traditional pattern of teaching and assessment was often not that effective.
- Increased class sizes have at least encouraged staff to reconsider how they teach and assess.
- The traditional British system effectively disbarred most people from higher education including many who would benefit from it. To an extent it has been the high costs of the traditional system with its high staff–student ratios and concern for absolute and culturally based conceptions of quality that made the costs of large scale expansion prohibitive to governments.
- Individuals and society at large would benefit from a large scale expansion of higher education. This could be achieved by redirecting resources from armaments and motorways. However we don't expect that to happen.
- The reality is that teachers and students are already under great pressure

because of increased enrolments etc. That pressure will increase. It won't go away by ignoring it.

- Unless significant change occurs staff and students will collapse in an attempt to keep the old system going. The result will be a dramatic decline in quality.
- If you care about quality but cannot increase resources then you have no option but to change methods.
- Perhaps the best we can do is to use radical change to slow down the decline in quality, but in so doing we can move to an effective system of mass higher education.
- What staff (and administrators) need now is practical advice and help on how to organise teaching, learning and assessment to cope with increased enrolments and class size. This book hopes to make a contribution to that aim.

The book's scope and organisation

In terms of the previous literature on class size this book adds to that small group of texts that are immediately addressed to the classroom teacher. Its rationale is similar to the American Sociological Association's compilation of articles on *Teaching the Mass Class* (McGee 1986, 1991). In the preface to that volume, Reece McGee argues that the mass class 'offers special problems that the normal class does not, and perhaps special opportunities as well, but also demands special procedures and preparation' (McGee, 1991, vi).

Weiner (1987) has edited a more general text on teaching large classes from a North American perspective while the Professional Development Centre at the University of New South Wales have brought together a wealth of short suggestions for teaching with reduced resources (Andresen 1988; Andresen *et al* 1989; Magin *et al* 1989). An annotated bibliography is to be found at the end of this volume, and references are given at the end of each chapter.

In Chapter Two, Andrew Ward and Alan Jenkins report on their research at Oxford Polytechnic on the problems faced by students and teachers in large classes. They show that for many students dominant experiences are bewilderment and feeling anonymous. For staff, central problems are feeling over-stressed and the course being out of their control.

In Chapter Three, Graham Gibbs systematically considers the problems faced by teachers and students in large classes. He sets out two broad strategies, to 'control' students and to give them 'independence', that teachers can use to design courses which seek to hold on to quality yet cope with large student numbers.

The bulk of the book consists of accounts by teachers who have significantly changed how they deliver the courses to cope with increased enrolments. The case studies exemplify a variety of possible solutions.

In Chapter Four, Alan Jenkins shows how, by changing the form of the traditional lecture to enable small group discussion within the lecture, students can feel individually responsible for their own learning and achieve levels of achievement more often associated with small discussion-based classes.

In Chapter Five, Nick Johnston reports on the experience of a group of law lecturers who, to cope with greatly increased enrolments, radically changed a lecture-based course, to one where much of the course content was delivered by workbooks written and designed by teaching staff.

In Chapter Six, Ken Howells and Sue Piggott re-designed an introductory physiology course with its mixture of lectures and discussion sections, to one that was designed around a comprehensive textbook. The new course adopted many of the features of the Keller system with its tightly specified teacher objectives, compulsory text and frequent testing. One of their concerns was to meet the needs of students with very different academic backgrounds. Large introductory courses tend to have students who are studying the course to satisfy very different disciplinary requirements.

In Chapter Seven, Ashley Green records the history of his attempts to re-design an introductory physics course to meet the diverse needs of physical science, engineering and geology students. His course now includes a variety of learning materials (workbooks, videos and computer courseware) to enable students to find different ways through the material to suit their needs. Additionally, despite a doubling in student numbers, he has managed to limit his assessment load by carefully analysing what are the key skills and knowledge that have to be assessed by him.

The next two case studies show in very different contexts how teachers can design courses that support student groups to take on some of the responsibility of teaching and assessing their peers.

In Chapter Eight, John Gold and Martin Haigh demonstrate that despite significantly worsening staff–student ratios they have managed to maintain fieldwork as a quality experience for students by helping them to be more independent of the staff and for much of their learning to be in small supportive groups. This case study reveals that staff have to structure courses carefully so that students can take on more independent and supportive roles.

Such is also a central underlying theme, in Chapter Nine, to Julie Hartley and Harinder Bahra's account of how they set up autonomous student support groups to meet the needs of part-time students in a business course.

These case studies are innovations by individual teachers or course teams from particular disciplines but in our judgement their underlying principles could be widely adopted by staff across a wide range of disciplines who are attempting to cope with large classes.

To an extent, individual lecturers and course teams in other institutions could make similar changes with only limited co-operation from immediate colleagues or the institution as a whole. However, some changes require action and support by a whole subject group or department and perhaps major changes at the level of the whole institution. For example, to write and publish a workbook-style course may require colleagues to co-operate to a common writing style and will require departmental and institutional funds and support to release some staff to write course materials, secretarial and design teams to produce them and a well equipped print-room that can produce the workbooks quickly and at little or no cost to the individual student. To enable this sort of development requires departments and institutions to make careful but at times ruthless strategic decisions.

These themes are developed in Chapter Ten by Frank Webster, who outlines a strategy developed by one subject group – that is to designate some courses as 'resource rich' in which students get much staff support including small group discussion and frequent feedback from assessment. To support these quality courses other courses are designated as 'resource poor' and are taught largely by large formal lectures and assessed entirely by unseen exams.

The development of these themes is continued in Chapter Eleven by Clive Booth and David Watson, who consider the all important role that key institutional decision makers can play in supporting and encouraging change. Without strong institutional support, teaching staff can only make limited progress in coping with increased student numbers.

In the concluding chapter, Chapter Twelve, Graham Gibbs and Alan Jenkins draw on these case studies to suggest general guidelines for anyone teaching larger classes with reduced resources and who cares about quality.

Most of the case studies are from Oxford Polytechnic. Evidently this reflects the fact that these were well known to us. We also consider it reflects credit on staff and administrators in that institution for their attention to quality teaching at higher SSRs. No doubt it also results from this institution's dominant modular course structure experiencing the stresses of large classes earlier than many other colleges in the UK. One benefit to the reader is that each case study need not spell out its particular institutional context – that of Oxford Polytechnic is described in the introduction to Chapter Two. Each chapter is written so that they are self contained and may be read in any order.

Beyond British higher education

Although this book is based on British experience of higher education, we consider that its message and suggestions can be adapted to others' experience. We also consider that many of its suggestions can be adapted by teachers in continental Europe, Australia, North America and elsewhere long accustomed to large classes. What is perhaps particular about some of the experiences reported is that many of the case studies seek to hold on to aspects of British conceptions of quality higher education but at very different staff–student ratios than was traditional in Britain and much closer to other mass education systems.

British teachers now need to learn from the experience of mass education systems; but perhaps we can contribute something in return – particularly where, as in the USA, Canada and elsewhere, there have been calls for greater attention to the quality of the undergraduate experience. We support the views of Ben Massey, President of the University of Maryland University College, who while opening the 1991 international conference on Improving University Teaching argued 'We have begun to think in terms of doing the best for the most, rather than the most for the best' (Proceedings, 1991, 5).

References

Andresen, L. W. (1988) *Lecturing to Large Groups: A Guide to Doing it Less But Better*. 2nd edition, Tertiary Education Research Centre, University of New South Wales.

Andresen, L. (1991) *The Influence of Class Size on Teaching and Learning Law at the University of New South Wales*. Professional Development Centre, University of New South Wales.

Andresen, L., Nightingale, P., Boud, D. and Magin, D. (1989) *Strategies for Assessing Students*. Professional Development Centre, University of New South Wales.

Association of University Teachers (1990) *Goodwill Under Stress*: Morale in UK Universities, London, AUT.

Department of Education and Science (1991) *Higher Education in the Polytechnics and Colleges*. Humanities and Social Sciences, London, HMSO.

Feldman, K. A. (1984) 'Class Size and College Students' Evaluations of Teachers and Courses', *Research in Higher Education*, 21 (4), 45-116.

Lindsay, R. and Paton-Saltzberg, R. (1987) 'Resource Changes and Academic Performance at an English Polytechnic', *Studies in Higher Education*, 12 (2), 213-27.

Magin, D., Nightingale, P., Andresen, L. and Boud, D. (1989) *Strategies for Increasing Students' Independence*. Professional Development Centre, University of New South Wales,.

McGee, R. (1986) (2nd edn 1991) *Teaching the Mass Class*. Washington, American Sociological Association.

McKeachie W. J. (1986) *Teaching Tips* . Lexington, D C Heath and Company.

Proceedings, (1991) *Improving University Teaching*. Seventeenth International Conference, Glasgow. Maryland, University of Maryland University College.

Smith, M. L. and Glass, G. V. (1980) 'Meta-analysis of Research on Class, Size and its Relationship to Attitudes and Instruction', *American Educational Research Journal*, 17 (4), 419-33.

University Grants Committee (1963) *Report of the Committee on Higher Education*. The Robbins Report, London, HMSO.

University Grants Committee (1964) *Report of the Committee on University Teaching Methods*. The Hale Report, London, HMSO.

Weimer, M. G. (1987) *Teaching Large Classes Well*. San Francisco, Jossey Bass.

Chapter 2

The problems of learning and teaching in large classes

Andrew Ward and Alan Jenkins

SUMMARY

This chapter reviews the changes in class size at Oxford Polytechnic which is the setting for most of the innovations in course design analysed in subsequent chapters. The central results of a research study on the problems faced by teachers and students in large classes are then discussed. For students the dominant problems are anonymity and passivity. For staff the dominant problems are not being able to relate to students as individuals and being overwhelmed by the number of demands placed upon them. The scale of these problems shows that radical changes are needed in the ways that courses are delivered.

A student described the experience of learning in a large class as being: 'like numbers at the end of a computer print-out'. A lecturer commented: 'I find it difficult to know individual students. This reinforces my feeling of performing rather than teaching.' A head of department said: 'We have lost staff . . . because they cannot face standing in front of large groups of people. Good teachers, good academics, have said "I can't do this". They were put in charge of big courses. They couldn't sleep at night, couldn't stop worrying about it. They just couldn't cope.'

This chapter is an account of problems of learning and teaching in large classes. We will report students' experiences of feeling bewildered, overwhelmed and anonymous. For staff the dominant feeling is being over-stressed, the demands of large classes taking them beyond that sense of being in control of a class.

We recognise that in many large classes, students and staff may enjoy and gain from the experience. Here our focus is on some of the problems for students and staff posed by large classes. Our concern is to bring out the experience of what happens when things go wrong. It is to show why an increase in class size requires teachers radically to reconsider how they deliver their courses.

This chapter is also very much an ethnographic study: a story of a particular group of staff and students in one place (Oxford Polytechnic) in a particular era (1983-91). Here we emphasise those aspects that we consider relevant to staff and students in other institutions. For example, we give limited attention to problems of campus and classroom overcrowding that may be specific to Oxford Polytechnic. However, for readers to make sense of what follows it is important to know something of the particular context of that institution.

A particular context: Oxford Polytechnic

Oxford Polytechnic is a medium-sized English Polytechnic mainly concerned with undergraduate education. Most of the courses are delivered in an American-style credit system – the Modular Course. Here students choose their own programme of study by selecting from about 1,000 modules (course units) available. Each module represents between one-third and one-quarter of a term's work for full-time students. Many modules are taught and assessed in one eleven-week term. A student progresses through the course by accumulating credits for each module passed.

Most Modular Course students study two 'fields' – a 'field' being roughly equivalent to an academic discipline such as Law or English. Others take a 'double field' which concentrates on a subject area such as Earth Sciences or Human Biology (Watson *et al*, 1989).

Government policy in the 1980s forced Oxford Polytechnic, like other UK institutions, to expand student numbers without related increases in staff. Some of the student increases were because of government pressure to expand those subjects considered more vocational, eg business studies. In June 1983, Graham Gibbs, then Head of the Educational Methods Unit, reported to the Polytechnic's key planning committee that the increased SSRs called for a radical reappraisal of teaching methods and structural changes throughout the institution. The report was strongly attacked by many staff as likely to justify and cause further cuts in staffing. Its recommendations were immediately shelved.

Though pressure of increased student numbers was felt throughout the institution, particular problems were faced by the Modular Course. The problems resulted from the efficiencies of scale of having introductory courses that were compulsory or acceptable to students from a variety of fields. This led to rapid increases in size for introductory modules in particular, together with a wider range of student backgrounds within modules. This is a central theme of Ashley Green's case study of teaching introductory physics (Chapter Seven). However the Modular Course also employs a comprehensive computer-based management system which provided a powerful statistical base for evaluating the course.

The impact of increased numbers or course or class size is shown in Table 2.1. As overall student numbers increased, particular increases were evident

Table 2.1 Numbers of Modules at Oxford Polytechnic of Different Size Registration in 1984–85 and 1990–91

No. of Students attending Module	1984-5	1990-91	% increase 1984-5 1990-91
0–60	545	717	31.5
61–100	64	110	71.8
101–180	22	66	200
181–400	0	13	α
Total no. of modules offered	631	906	36.7

Note: Modules were first categorised 0–20, 21–40, 41–60 etc. and then re-categorised where there appeared clear changes in the data.

in classes with over 60 students; and while in 1984–85 there had been no courses with over 180 students enrolled, by 1990–91 there were 13 such courses. These increases in class size were greater than the overall increase in SSR, illustrating a general phenomenon. In order to cope with increased student numbers, class sizes are having to increase very rapidly. It is simply not possible only to increase the number of classes or even to keep increases in class size in line with overall SSRs. Students had to adjust to changes in class size, and staff had to solve the new problems of teaching large classes.

Throughout much of this period the academic head (Dean) of the Modular Course was David Watson (see also Chapter Eleven). His leadership helped initiate two evaluation studies that sought to monitor the impact of class size and suggest solutions. Capitalising on the Modular Course's strong statistical base Roger Lindsay and Renee Paton-Saltzberg studied the impact of resource changes on student performance (see Chapter One).

In 1988 David Watson initiated a different but related study to carry out an action-research study to recommend ways of ameliorating the problems of increasing student–staff ratios (SSR). The brief was as follows: 'An investigation of current and potential training methods for basic modules (ie first-year courses) in all disciplines with enrolments of 80-plus students; to include the identification of current good practice, relevant staff-development strategies, and proposals for the organisation of space, equipment and other resources.'

As is discussed in Chapter One, definitions of 'a large class' are somewhat arbitrary. The figure of 80 enrolled students was decided by the Dean in discussion with heads of department and others and evidently reflected staff perceptions at Oxford Polytechnic at that time. The eventual in-house report contained 29 recommendations and many detailed suggestions (Jenkins and Ward, 1989).

Many of the recommended strategies were teaching and assessment methods that staff throughout the institution had adopted and developed to cope successfully with problems posed by increased class size. Some of these strategies are detailed in the case studies that follow. But, to repeat, our focus here is on the problems that large classes pose to students and staff at

Oxford Polytechnic which we consider relevant to staff and students elsewhere. As with any ethnographic study readers are asked to read our report critically in the light of their own experience and knowledge.

Methodology

Sixty first-year modules with 80 plus students were targeted for investigation and research was conducted in the first two terms of the 1988–89 academic year. Several data sources were used for our conclusions here. We investigated both student and staff perceptions.

Halfway through the first term, students from a large Geography module were invited to a group discussion on the problems of large classes. These students had experience of two or three other large classes. All students of that particular Geography module were also given a questionnaire in week nine of the first term. This helped to gauge whether the problems were temporary. More focussed questionnaires were also administered to large introductory Economics and English modules. Further group discussions were held with second-year student representatives from a variety of disciplines who were asked to reflect on their experience of large first-year classes. In addition, Student Union officials were interviewed and a number of large classes were systematically observed.

A questionnaire was sent to staff responsible for the 60 targeted large modules. Respondents were asked to list and describe three problems caused by the large number of students on the module. The questionnaire also asked for descriptions of special teaching strategies used for large modules and descriptions of issues the Polytechnic's administration should tackle. Replies were received from 52 staff, a response rate of 87 per cent. Some of these teaching staff were interviewed.

A progress report was made at a feedback seminar attended by over 70 staff. Three months later, about 50 staff attended a second feedback seminar; they were divided into groups to discuss the problems and strategies highlighted by our interim report. Although the prime purpose of this second feedback seminar was to allow staff an input into our eventual recommendations, it also brought clearer statements from staff about the problems of teaching large classes, and therefore added to our data.

Problems of large classes for students

The reality is different from expectations

At Oxford Polytechnic, and probably elsewhere, the largest classes are introductory first-year courses where students are new to the institution and usually new to higher education.

What class size do first-year students expect? We were struck by how unprepared first-year students were for the size of class they were required to deal with. Few had been forewarned either formally or informally, and the prospectus at that time ignored the issue. Based on high school experiences, students expected less than 30 in their class, whereas they usually got over 100. We quantified this sudden shift in class size by asking students in three modules (in Geography, English and Economics) to tell us the size of their A-level class if they had taken the subject at A-level (the national exam generally taken in their final year in high school).

The median A-level class size was 12 for both English and Geography and 14 for Economics. Only five of the 146 students answering the question had A-level classes over 30, and none higher than 36. The sizes at the Polytechnic were 137 (Economics), 144 (English), and 103 (Geography) (Jenkins & Ward, 1990). One of our recommendations was that the Polytechnic ensured that its promotional literature advised students clearly on what to expect. These large classes initially generated feelings associated with sudden change. Students commented on being uncomfortable and confused. Some spent their first weeks in a state of shock: 'I found some of them [large classes] overwhelming. The size of this place and the number of people was totally overwhelming.' Others knew what to expect but were still affected: 'I had friends who'd been to universities and had told me there were lecture theatres and that, but when you actually get here and find large lectures, it's a bit daunting.' One student who had 16 in her A-level Geography class told us that by the end of the first term she had adjusted to large classes: 'I now feel relatively blasé. I hardly notice the number.' Another student from the same class stated: 'I'm beginning to get used to it, but I still think smaller classes are more effective.'

Other problems of expectation are not caused directly by large classes but are aggravated by them. In higher education students need to look after themselves more. 'You weren't organised', said one student, 'you were expected to do everything on your own.' Another agreed: 'It was different from school, where everything is done for you.' These students expected lecturers to help as much as schoolteachers had. The concept of a 'personal tutor' was unfathomable to one student, who politely suggested that the correct term was 'impersonal tutor': 'I thought we'd get a better relationship with personal tutors, and we'd be able to talk about different aspects of the course, as you go through.'

Forming relationships

Students need to form relationships with staff and with other students, particularly students from their own subject, in order to feel part of the institution and to develop a formal and informal environment essential to learning. Yet students frequently told us of the anonymity of large classes:

> You don't know many people. Okay, there's the people in the seminar group, but there's no way you can get to know everybody. I mean, [turns to another student in the discussion] I've never seen *you* before.

Well, you just don't get to know anybody. You know, you walk in and its very daunting, all the numbers sitting in there. Then you just go and sit next to your friends, who you just sort of know, and you stay in your groups and you feel just numbers really, at the end of a computer print-out.

At school I was used to 16 people [in the class] with the teacher knowing them not only by name, but by character and consequently knowing how to treat each one to get the best out of them.

Early in the year, students drop out of classes, and remaining students find it difficult to recognise faces in the changing gallery of their peer group. To one student: 'It seemed like you were in a different class each time.' But that same student also admitted that by the sixth week: 'It's a lot better now you know people.' In a large gathering, students have less courage to ask questions and often remain in a passive role.

I mean, if you're in a lecture with 200 people for three hours a week, you don't know anybody at the end of it. So by the end of that week there are 200 faces that you still don't know. Not only can you not speak in lectures – or you're not supposed to – you've got to sit there stone-faced and take down what he's saying (or she, as the case may be). You never get to know anyone.

It would be nice to ask questions occasionally but the size of the group makes this embarrassing.

As we have seen, students' relationships with their personal tutors are rarely personal – except when faced with major problems. Even then, it may need persistence:

If you are bothered about what you are actually doing and what's going on, and things aren't going right, you have to go there [to see your personal tutor]. I remember when I first got here. On the first day they'd processed my timetable totally wrong – all the wrong modules – and on the first day after enrolment day I sat up by that office for about three hours waiting.

Relationships with lecturers and module leaders also form slowly, yet this is a time when students may need reassurance:

You could be going in the wrong direction. No real feedback till you get your work done, and then you've failed your exam and failed your module.

Organisation

A predominant impression of the students we investigated was of bewilderment and anonymity and of not finding a clear structure in which to learn. We recognise this was for many a result of being new to college and away from home for the first time. But clearly it was also caused or accentuated by the anonymity and lack of clear direction of many large classes. Students' comments also gave us a sense of what they wanted in large classes. They liked lecturers to be organised and approachable, with lecturers setting goals to suit the stress of large classes at the start of term:

> I also found that the modules that I got on better with were the ones where they didn't try to pack in everything they could on the subject. They made the basic points, or the important points, and made sure that by the time you left the lecture you understood them. You might come out and think, 'Well, hang on a minute, we only learned about two things.' But that was a good foundation for you to then go away, look at whatever seminar sheet or hand-outs. That's a lot better than coming out totally confused by the wealth of information that they try to cram in, and they cram it in in such a way that you can't possibly listen and take notes at times, 'cos they are just rabbiting on.

Many large courses were taught by a variety of lecturers and with multiple parallel seminar or laboratory groups. Students commented on the confused and conflicting instructions they received:

> There's too much variance in one module between different seminar leaders. With one they might say, 'Right, you've got to have this essay on this day.' And the next one, 'Okay, you're supposed to have it in by this day, but, if you don't, okay, you can give it to me tomorrow.' Or, 'That's not relevant to the course, you don't have to do it if you don't want to.'

An invaluable aid to structure is something to pull the course together, such as a course reader or course workbook: 'It's chaos, but just manageable because there is the structure of the workbook. Without it people would panic.' When asked how he would describe a lecturer who had good organisation skills, one student gave the following reply: 'Somebody who was able to say at the beginning where the course was going, where the direction of the course is going, what they expect of it, what they expect you to learn, to get out of the course. And how they were going to go about that. Give you a kind of direction for the future.'

Problems of large classes for staff

Forming relationships

'Teaching is about relationships,' said one lecturer in a feedback seminar. 'Staff, like students, have more difficulty forming relationships in large classes.' This view was supported by questionnaire responses:

> Large numbers plus one-term modules mean staff hardly get to know

most students and vice versa. Construction of any sort of relationship, the basis of best teaching, is therefore impossible.

A two-way problem between students and staff in getting to know each other and developing a rapport. I see this as a problem of staff not communicating in a way that is most effective/meaningful to the students and that students may feel unable to approach staff with problems/issues that arise from sessions.

However, the relationship problem takes a different form for staff. Whereas students usually know a lecturer's name, the staff have difficulty recognising students and learning names. Shy students may become invisible in large classes, and indeed one lecturer commented on how impossible it was to get to know the students except: 'the good, the bad and the ugly (or at least the loud-mouthed)'. It is a setting which suits performers, both on stage and in the audience:

I find it difficult to know individual students. This reinforces my feeling of performing rather than teaching. I am certain the students want to be known as individuals.

The shyer students, who might have the confidence to contribute in small groups, tend to keep quiet in large ones.

Staff need to know how students are progressing, but this is harder if they cannot put a face to the name. However, if students do try to establish relationships outside of the classroom, it may lead to a further problem for staff with too many students knocking on doors:

I often feel that all problems come back to the module leader and with so many students doing the course there always appears to be someone wanting something sorted out. Even though many student problems are effectively sorted out by others teaching the course, I seem to find that my day is repeatedly disrupted.

The time taken to deal with individual problems is out of all proportion to the time allowed for the module. There are additional staff to help but the problem still remains.

The dynamics of communication may be unsettling for staff, and this is aggravated if seminar groups take time to settle down or if students taking a module are from different backgrounds: 'The students come from at least 15 modular fields, so examples used must either be very simple and under-standable to all or be relevant to a few fields only (maybe only one).' Some staff agreed with students' criticisms of 'impersonal tutors', although, for staff, this issue was submerged among other issues.

Organisation

Just as most students appreciate a clear sense of organisation and direction to a course, so do staff. Many saw it as a central requirement for a large course but often more difficult to establish:

> I think most students require a clear sense of the goals of a course and where they are heading. I also believe strongly in being somewhat unpredictable, responding to events and particular students. In my advanced course with 20 to 30 students there is a lot of negotiation between me and students and within the students as a group as to the direction and assessment of a course and what is to happen within sessions. Many class sessions are created there and then.

> I take a totally different approach to my large introductory module. It often feels like I am preparing for a large-scale expedition. I start months beforehand getting all the hand-outs and resources ready. There is a tremendous attention to detail and double-checking every-thing. Are enough copies of key texts in the library, will enough copies of the textbook be in the book shop before term begins? The course guide is gone through carefully to make sure all the organisational details re assessment etc are clearly and unambiguously stated so I don't have students continually asking me as to what is required of them. All sessions are carefully planned well beforehand and I try to get most of the hand-outs printed before term begins. I find it quite stressful and at times exhilarating. But, in the past year or so, increased numbers, unpredictable enrolments and battling to get adequate rooms has made life hell.

Many staff had responded to the organisational problems of large classes by producing workbooks. Their form varied but they often contained details on assignments and key reading. The size ranged from a few pages to over 600 pages for the Introduction to Law course (see Chapter Five). Workbooks bring problems the publishing industry would recognise – the need for desk-top publishing skills, typing log-jams, print-run forecasts, printing delays and erratic distribution to students, who may or may not attend lectures:

> As numbers increase so do the printing costs and the need to keep printing extra copies to cope. This is especially true of large modules. It is helpful to know exact student numbers a term ahead at least as this is how the print room scheduling timetable works.

> The production is a major item for the print room. I have to judge the likely numbers. If I get it wrong I will either have a room full of unused booklets or armies of workbookless students beating on my door. The Polytechnic should be offering an integrated desk-top publishing service to the likes of me. I've learnt the editorial skills the hard way.

Module leaders are more likely to need extra staff for large modules, and therefore need to find them, brief them and reward them. The extra staff may not know the course material as well as the module leader, who may therefore need to develop skills of a course manager. Extra staff may raise the problem of inconsistency, noted earlier by students and recognised by some members of staff: 'Problem one – co-ordinating all the staff on the module so that each group of students in seminars, etc have the same kind of course. Rumours flourish among students because of this.'

Another course leader observed in one introductory course:

I have got 23 seminar groups. I have got 23 tutors. Now I have to write to them about marking. In one of our advanced modules which has 24 tutors the only way we have got the seminars to work well is for the seminar tutors to sit in on the lectures. Now that apparently gives many members of staff more hassle than anything else, the fact that their colleagues, their peers are observing them. It also raises the problem that the lecturer will try to impress their colleagues rather than teach the students.

Large classes have higher noise levels and may start late by the time all the students are finally settled. A lecturer arriving early will find the room occupied by a prior class, then crowded by students milling for the current class. There is no opportunity to check the room beforehand. The larger the class, the more difficult the organisation of any outdoor visits – to schools (for education modules) or field sites (eg for biology and planning):

Visits to schools and to anywhere outside the Poly become difficult to do. You have to go further and wider to find places willing to accept them; the expense and logistics become very difficult and takes hours and hours of staff time.

Teaching Methods

Faced with organisational problems and problems of getting to know students, staff are led progressively towards a problem that troubles them more – choosing the most appropriate teaching methods. When we allowed staff at a feedback seminar to choose one of six problems for group discussion, almost half of those present gravitated towards the problem of 'teaching methods'. The precursors to this problem have been hinted at above – finding the right level, meeting the needs of students of differing backgrounds, dealing with high noise levels, launching a workbook, becoming a course manager, dealing with inflexible room furniture and the aggravation of arranging outside visits. Other precursors are explained below – declining library and material resources, increasing stress levels, etc – and these too provoke the thought that solutions are dependent on changing teaching methods.

The absence of microphones makes me hoarse, front-row students deaf and overseas students' problems worse.

> Teaching a class of a hundred plus is difficult. I find it impossible to give student tasks as there is too much chatting/undiscipline. I therefore have to keep to lecturing with a short break in the middle.

Stated simply, the problem is choosing teaching methods which minimise all the other inherent problems, ie organisation, forming relationships, assessment and evaluation, library and computer resources. Lectures rely on good acoustics. Group work has problems of control. Seminars, tutorials and practicals seem to beg more staff or more resources. And workbooks call for new skills. Above all, there is the need to change but there is the fear that experiments may fail and the knowledge that most students desire structure and routine.

In the early 1980s throughout the institution there had been considerable experiment in teaching methods. Though traditional lectures and teacher-led seminars still had their place, many courses had moved to much more student-centred teaching and learning methods. However, under pressures of numbers, many staff felt they reluctantly had to go back to more traditional methods, a theme to which we will return when discussing assessment. Here is one teacher's first experience of lecturing to over 300 students:

> I did experiment for the first two weeks. I tried to make the class somewhat interactive. I then decided I would soldier on with the straight lecture which I am really not very happy with, but couldn't come up with anything else. I tried making the class interactive but I just couldn't cope with it. If students were talking to me I just couldn't hear them. I couldn't make out which students were speaking. The only ones talking to me were in the first five rows and there was this great mass in the back. In the end I decided that the conventional lecture was the best educational experience I could deliver under the constraints. That's what worries me.

Assessment

In the years prior to our study, many staff at Oxford Polytechnic – as elsewhere – had significantly changed how they assessed courses. In the 1970s unseen exams were dominant, forming 100 per cent of the assessment on the module. By the end of 1980s there had been considerable development and experimentation. Coursework, in the form of essays, laboratory reports, groups projects and spoken presentations had come to dominate the pattern of student assessment.

These had been introduced because staff felt they stimulated students to more effective learning. But by the time of our study many staff felt the pressure of student numbers on large courses meant they had to reconsider assessment quite radically and neglect what they thought educationally desirable or else be swamped by the workload. One area particularly under threat was coursework, as staff felt overwhelmed by the volume of marking required. As one lecturer put it: 'Marking 160 scripts is not a pleasant way of passing a week-end!' Others stated: 'Written work is not compulsory now, again to save on staff hours. Assessment is 100 per cent by final exam. Again not ideal,' and 'Coursework has to be quick to mark. I only take in numerical tables, graphics (maps) and booking sheets for assessment. Written reports are out!'

Similarly, staff may feel overwhelmed by what they think they should be doing when assessing student work, eg giving useful, comprehensive feedback and setting important tasks: 'I don't carefully mark some assignments – though I don't tell the students.'

The problems of marking exams are aggravated by the necessary rapid turn-round. Reliability and validity also become issues, whether one lecturer takes on an increased load or more staff (and detailed marking schemes) are involved in the marking process: 'The sheer weight of marking and the short time allowed to produce exam marks may make the quality of marking less good'; 'Marking becomes an enormous task and therefore again I have split the marking between three members of staff. The problem is to maintain an even standard. Also there are limits on the amount of written work set. Its difficult to be consistent.' It is also far more difficult for staff to spot plagiarism or cheating.

Another lecturer commented: 'The main problems are time for coursework marking and time for exam marking. I divide the practicals into four coursework assignments, and I like to get these back with a one-week turn-around. This causes great pressure in those particular weeks (I like to get them back so students know their mistakes before the next practical).'

Some solutions to assessment problems – multiple-choice questions, computer-based marking etc. – may bring their own problems of learning new skills.

Library and Computer Resources

Larger classes had led to overload in the library, forcing decisions between multiple copies of a key textbook or single copies of a variety of texts. A lecturer commented:

Too many students chasing too few copies of key texts. Library (and field) are opposed to buying too many multiple copies.

Large numbers create a rush on the library's stocks. Putting things on 'restricted loan' helps, but is still a problem when 160 people need to consult the same book at once.

The library does not have enough copies of books and journal articles for the student to do the 'extra' reading around a topic.

Obvious solutions – workbooks containing key readings and books kept in the department – may produce other problems, in particular those of space, access and security. One lecturer explained that he kept photocopies of the most popular articles in the department but 'students steal these, the same with my personal books'.

Many first-year courses have developed group projects that require students to develop their understanding of an issue by finding relevant information in the library. Again these group projects in large introductory courses have been developed for sound educational reasons but also to take some of the load off the teaching staff. However, poorly planned or poorly resourced projects just pass the burden on to the library staff: 'The library is now having to assist first-year students with literature searching, and this term in particular it has been noticeable that the preparation of bibliographies is being required as early as the first week, despite the student having no knowledge of sources or searching skills.'

The issue of library opening hours was raised at a feedback seminar after a few North American solutions to large-class problems had been put forward as potential solutions in Britain. One lecturer commented that North American solutions might be fine in Britain if North American resources came with them and libraries were open 24 hours a day (as they are on some North American campuses): 'We mustn't make suggestions in isolation', she said.

Practicals or workshops may not be worth continuing because of lack of resources. As one lecturer remarked on computing practicals: 'Two students per terminal reduces the effectiveness of these sessions.' A second lecturer picked up a more subtle problem: 'the slow response of the PRIME network when many users are logged in'.

The computer-resource problem was described by two other lecturers:

Twenty to twenty-five workstations involving about six tutors. Because of the large number of students the software/hardware facilities are stretched to the limit and often cause problems and difficulties. This being a first-year, first-term module, students demand a lot of attention from the tutors.

The computer resources are swamped by students waiting till the last minute to meet coursework deadlines.

Health

As indicated by the head of department quoted at the beginning of this chapter, staff may lose sleep worrying about large classes. They may perceive either a loss of control or a threat to their standards. Teaching large classes can be very stressful and we found no shortage of comment on the overload of work involved:

Large numbers of seminars mean more tutorials for more staff. This means the staff get exhausted quicker.

One year I had to run another module, for the first time as well, in the same term and nearly collapsed.

Two of us who teach this module should be devoting 40 per cent of our time to this but we have so many other demands on our time now that it is very difficult to do this. We work excessively hard to keep the thing going.

Conclusion

We have shown that for students and staff the experience of large classes can be fraught with difficulties. Most first-year students experience large classes and are often unprepared for and bewildered by them. Students frequently talked about being anonymous and passive and are frustrated by their lack of say in what is happening to them.

Relatedly, staff can feel hemmed in by not being able to relate to students as individuals. They can find themselves driven back to traditional teaching and assessment methods, eg the lecture and 100 per cent unseen exam. Staff, particularly those most responsible for teaching and organising a large class, can feel overwhelmed by the organisational problems and assessment demands. And all this takes place at a time when staff are under increasing pressure to publish and undertake consultancy.

The focus of this chapter has been on the problems of large classes, as perceived by the students and staff at one institution. While drafting the chapter we were concerned that too much emphasis on problems might be not only negative but unfair on Oxford Polytechnic staff who have responded so successfully to the challenge of large classes. However, accounts of good practice in coping with large classes can be found in the following chapters and so we feel that it is justified to make a clear statement of the problems at this stage. By stressing these problems we hope that teachers and administrators will recognise the need radically to reconsider course delivery methods. Without such a radical approach the quality of experience of both students and staff will suffer.

Acknowledgements

We wish to thank the many students and staff who participated in this project, Liz Beaty of Brighton Polytechnic who acted as a consultant and the typists who produced such accurate transcripts of interviews.

References

Jenkins, A. and Ward, A. (1989) *Teaching Large Classes: Modular Course Evaluation Project, 1988-9*. Oxford, Oxford Polytechnic internal report.

Jenkins, A. and Ward, A. (1990) 'Economical with the truth? Promotional information for prospective geography students', *Journal of Geography in Higher Education*, 14 (2), 182-7.

Watson, D. *et al* (1989) Managing the Modular Course: Perspectives from Oxford Polytechnic. Milton Keynes, Society for Research into Higher Education and the Open University Press.

Chapter 3
Control and independence

Graham Gibbs

SUMMARY

This chapter examines two broad strategic options for replacing the conventional patterns of teaching and learning in higher education in the UK in order to cope more effectively with large classes. It examines the nature of these conventional patterns and the problems associated with them as student numbers increase. For each of the areas of problems it then contrasts 'control' and 'independence' strategies for dealing with them and gives examples of the teaching, learning and assessment methods associated with each of these strategies. Finally it discusses the ways in which these strategies can be mixed, and looks ahead to the extent to which and the ways in which these strategies are adopted in the case studies in the chapters that follow.

Introduction

In examining the broad options facing teaching and learning in the face of larger classes it is helpful to examine the nature of course patterns they might replace. Course design and teaching methods employed in higher education in the UK are extraordinarily uniform in nature. While the variation is increasing, the broad pattern of students' experience of courses is still largely predictable. This pattern developed at a time when resources were relatively copious and the number of students per teacher was a half or even one-third of what it is today.

Course descriptions, if they existed at all, consisted of lists of topics. The content of weekly lectures overlapped with topic lists to some extent. There was reasonably frequent personal contact with students, individually or in small groups, frequent assignments for the purpose of giving feedback to students (usually in the form of essays or lab reports) and infrequent testing (usually in the form of a series of three-hour unseen exams taken only after several years of study). Students spent relatively little time in class (though as much as 100 per cent more in Engineering than in English) and were assumed to spend a great deal of time reading and studying independently, often in well-stocked libraries with plenty of space. Class sizes were frequently very small, but even where they were not it was possible for regular tutorial work to be undertaken in groups of six or so.

Whether or not this pattern ever really worked, it was adopted by the new and rapidly expanding universities and by the new public sector institutions. In polytechnics and colleges of higher education, especially those with strong further education roots, it was assumed that students were less able to work independently. As a result, the total quantity of class contact hours, and in particular the number of lectures, were higher than in Universities, often 50 to 100 per cent higher. Twenty years later, students in polytechnics still spend more time in class than do their university counterparts. Polytechnic and college libraries, and library stocks for newly emerging disciplines, were less well able to support 'reading for a degree' and there was less space available for independent study.

By the start of the 1990s the reality of students' experience was already a long way from the comfortable assumptions of the seventies. Lectures dominated and individual and small group tutoring had become less frequent and less effective due to class sizes. Coursework assignments also had become less frequent and were mainly used as tests rather than as learning opportunities. As student numbers increased neither capital funding, for building classrooms or study spaces, nor revenue, for stocking libraries, kept pace with these increases. The system was being required to teach more students without more resources, and class sizes soared. At the same time there were increased expectations on lecturers to spend more time on other activities and, by implication, less time on their teaching. They were pressured, by institutional reviews, by research rating exercises and by appraisal, to undertake more research, even though there was less research funding available to pay for their time. Lecturers were expected to be entrepreneurial and bring in consultancy, develop short courses for industry and the professions, and respond enthusiastically to a plethora of new initiatives such as the Training Agency's 'Enterprise in Higher Education' programme.

The extraordinary thing about this period of change is that teaching and learning methods and course patterns did not accommodate the increased class sizes, reduced resources and the ever more thinly stretched time and energy of lecturers. If the traditional pattern had ever worked, it had done so only through being oiled by easy and frequent individual exchanges between teacher and student. Ineffective lectures could be compensated for by brief individual explanations. Alternative sources of reading could be suggested when libraries were inadequate, or alternative essay topics negotiated. Students could be encouraged where student motivation had been ignored in course design, and guided where courses were vague as to their content and purpose. However one of the most prominent experiences of both students and lecturers in the new large classes has been that such informal exchange has all but disappeared. The traditional pattern has broken down, its inherent weaknesses now exposed. The weaknesses are now so extensive and so prominent that the pretence is no longer sustainable.

The most obvious negative consequences of increased class size within conventional course structures are summarised in Table 3.1. Each traditional area of activity, such as lectures or reading, is changing and bringing with it new problems.

Strategic options

Faced with this situation, what are the options? Until recently most lecturers, and most courses, have tried to ignore the problems and carry on much as before: trimming tutorials, cutting out options and reducing choice, increasing seminar size to 25 or 30, even splitting lecture classes of 500 into two classes of 250 in order to fit them into the largest room available, accepting narrower reading and tolerating regurgitation in exams by awarding lower-second-class degrees for it. Those elements of student experience from which quality has flowed have been steadily removed but there are no plans other than to continue the inexorable process of stripping courses bare. Lecturers have run themselves into the ground to keep the old regime alive. I believe that it is simply not possible to retain acceptable quality, to achieve remotely equivalent aims as in the past, with conventional methods. The conventional pattern of teaching and learning is no longer viable.

To continue with conventional methods, out of stubbornness, fear or ignorance of alternatives, and to accept the limited outcomes this would achieve, would be to accept defeat. New aims, down this path, mean lower aims. This is also politically unacceptable. Institutions, their validating and audit bodies, and their funding bodies would rather pretend that the old aims were being achieved than be honest and accept, and state, lower but achievable aims.

It would be possible to retain the old notions of what a course consisted of and adopt new ways of trying to achieve these aims. We believe that the majority of innovation at present is of this kind. Its goal is survival – to hold on to as much of the past as possible by adopting a few new methods. These methods are borrowed from mass teaching systems such as the Open University's distance teaching and much undergraduate teaching in the USA. As we shall see, this may allow survival, but it has an uphill task achieving the old aims.

Finally, it is possible to be more radical. Those aspects of traditional courses which have been most valued involve discussion, reflection, independent learning guided by tutors and wide reading. The focus has been on the role of the tutor in supporting this quality learning. Radical approaches attempt to retain this quality without the tutor being central in the same way. Students take over many of the traditional tutor roles and supervise each other and themselves in an atmosphere of independence and freedom. The goals of such processes are inevitably different. They are more diverse and arise more from students than from teachers. They place a greater emphasis on process and on learning to learn and less emphasis on content.

Table 3.1 Problems caused by large classes

Method	What has happened	Resulting problems
Lectures	Classes much larger	Difficult for students to ask questions. Difficult for lecturers to know if students understand. Difficult to elicit student answers. Due to lack of other contact, lecture notes need to be self-contained and complete, encouraging dictation. Difficult to encourage interaction between students.
	Lecture rooms bigger	Heightened problems of acoustics, visibility and attention.
Seminars	Groups much bigger	Students don't know each other. Tutor doesn't know the students. Easy for students to 'hide' and not take part. Difficult to respond to individuals. Low student participation. Little opportunity for individuals to pursue interests. Participation dominated by tutor and a few students. Poor preparation due to inadequate library provision. High absenteeism tolerated or not noticed.
	Less frequent meetings	Students do not get to know each other. Lack of group cohesion or momentum. Poor links with lectures and course work. As there is more material to be dealt with, discussion is superficial or very selective.
	Multiple seminar splits in parallel groups	Lack of consistency of content. Quality control poor. Stale, bored tutors. Scheduling problems.
Reading	Fewer books per student	Less reading, less relevant reading, patchy reading in the library.
	Students unable to afford books	Narrower focus, particularly in lectures and seminars which aim to cover ground the textbooks cover.
	Narrower range of books	Narrower, predictable reading. Predictable essays.
	Single copy of reference material (e.g. journals, Law Reports)	Journals become unrealistic source for students.
	Library space limited	Reading discouraged.
	Study space limited	Overcrowded coffee lounges used for reading.

Table 3.1 Continued

Method	What has happened	Resulting problems
Essays and assignments	Fewer and less frequent	Less practice at writing. Less preparation for exams. Smaller proportion of course material studied in depth. Encourages 'selective negligence'. Students put in fewer learning hours. Lack of momentum and pacing to study. Rarer essays become more anxiety provoking.
	Shorter	Develops different skills. Less emphasis on collating evidence into coherent arguments.
	Less feedback	Less learning. Less improvement in essay-writing.
Laboratories	Class size larger	Less hands-on experience. Experience of only part of a procedure. Less supervision. Labs often more limited and routine.
	Lab splits/repeats	Scheduling and timing problems in relation to lecture programme. Lecturers stale.
	Lab reports reduced	Less feedback on skill. Less link between theory and practice. Writing skills not developed.
	More routine labs	Experimental design skills not developed. Students bored.
Practical work	Too little equipment	Familiarity with equipment limited.
	Fewer field trips	Theory not linked with experience.
	Less time with equipment	Insufficient practice.
Creative work	Less supervision and guidance	Students develop more slowly and waste effort.
	Less time in the studio	Less hands-on experience, or isolated learning.
	Crowded studios	Uncongenial learning environment.
	Shared studios	No personalised learning space. Time wasted setting up work.
Supervised project and dissertation work	Less negotiation and clarification of project	Lack of direction and sense of ownership of project.
	Less supervision and encouragement	Less focussed and productive student effort.
	Limited access to resources	Narrower, shallower projects and frustrated students.
	Less feedback on work in progress	Less development of skills.
Problem classes	Larger classes	Less individual time with tutors. More time wasted while 'stuck'.
	Fewer classes	Less continuity and progression. Skills not reinforced, leading to problems later.

Table 3.1 Continued

Method	What has happened	Resulting problems
One-to-one tutorials	Fewer and shorter	Insufficient diagnosis of learning difficulties.
		Insufficient 'modelling' of academic reasoning and problem-solving.
		Lack of interaction and discussion in student learning.
	Tutors hard to contact	Students unable to progress and lose motivation.
		Serious student problems not picked up in time.

In order to contrast the options of control and independence we need to look at the way they address the main areas of difficulty faced by conventional courses with large classes.

Areas of difficulty

If we analyse the problems identified in Chapter Two, eight main areas of difficulty stand out:

1. *Lack of clarity of purpose*
   It is insufficiently clear to students what a course consists of: what is to be learnt, what is the purpose of specific assignments or reading, what an acceptable outcome of learning would look like. Conventional courses achieve a degree of clarity of purpose not through design, but through informal face-to-face contact. When this is reduced to a minimum, students lose direction. Lectures have never worked well to clarify purpose and the trend back to a reliance on lecturing has only highlighted the difficulty.

2. *Lack of knowledge about progress*
   Students need to know how they are doing: whether they are working hard enough, understand things adequately and are generally keeping up. As the number of assignments and tutorials drops and tutor feedback declines, so students lose this crucial sense of how they are doing. There is a much greater chance of them getting seriously behind or of progressing while unaware of serious flaws in their understanding or competence. This tends to lead to higher failure and drop-out rates and a good deal of anguish.

3. *Lack of advice on improvement*
   Even if students know they are not doing as well as is expected of them they still need to know what to do about it – how to improve. In large classes if students receive any advice it tends to be rather general in nature,

addressed to the whole class, concerning the most common problems. There is a lack of individualised, specific, help.

4. *Inability to support wide reading*
Conventional courses require extensive library resources. Two hundred students being required to 'read around' this week's topic stretches libraries well beyond their ability to cope. As a result students read less, and less widely.

5. *Inability to support independent study*
Traditional project and dissertation work involves one-to-one tutorial support and individual practical or laboratory work. This is becoming increasingly difficult to sustain and students are frequently left for long periods without adequate guidance and assistance.

6. *Lack of opportunity for discussion*
In large classes student learning is becoming solitary. The negotiation of meaning and exploration of half-formed ideas which discussion offers is being denied students.

7. *Inability to cope with variety of students*
At a time when the variety of student backgrounds has never been great, the ability of tutors to respond flexibly to students through personal contact has been taken away. Students are being treated as a homogeneous mass.

8. *Inability to motivate students*
Motivation has in the past come from personal contact with lecturers and involvement in small group discussion. When students' imagination was fired, library and other resources could give it free rein. In large classes, in the absence of either personal contact or small groups, and with inadequate resources to fuel motivation, students are frequently disengaged and passive.

Control and independence

There are two highly contrasting sets of strategies for dealing with these difficulties. One is to control the situation, and the other is to allow students freedom and independence. The best way to explain this difference is to examine the kinds of methods adopted by these two strategies for tackling each of these difficulties. These are summarised in Table 3.2 and then elaborated in more detail. This is not an exhaustive list, but is used to illustrate the strategies.

Control strategies

Problem 1: Lack of clarity of purpose

The control strategy involves the teacher defining the purpose of courses,

Area of difficulty resulting from large classes	Characteristic methods adopted	
	'Control' strategies	'Independence' strategies
1. Lack of clarity of purpose	a) Use of objectives b) Highly structured courses	a) Use of learning contracts b) Problem-based learning
2. Lack of knowledge of progress	a) Objective testing b) Programmed instruction and CAL	a) Development of student judgement b) Self-assessment
3. Lack of advice on improvement	a) Assignment attachment forms b) Automated tutorial feedback	a) Peer feedback and assessment
4. Inability to support reading	a) Use of set books b) Use of learning packages	a) Development of students' research skills b) More varied assignments
5. Inability to support independent study	a) Structured projects b) Lab guides	a) Group work b) Learning teams
6. Lack of opportunity for discussion	a) Structured lectures b) Structured seminars/ workshops	a) Student-led seminars b) Team assignments
7. Inability to cope with variety of students	a) Pre-tests plus remedial material b) Self-paced study (PSI)	a) Variety of support mechanisms b) Negotiated goals
8. Inability to motivate students	a) Frequent testing b) High failure rates	a) Engaging learning tasks b) Co-operative learning

Table 3.2 'Control' and 'Independence' strategies for dealing with difficulties resulting from large classes

classes and assignments in advance, in some detail, and in designing learning activities so that they tie in very closely with these pre-defined purposes.

a) *Use of objectives*: Objectives are statements of what should have been achieved on completion of a course of study. Behavioural objectives state these achievements in terms of the behaviour you would want to be able to observe in your students. For example:

At the end of this chapter readers should be able to:
  i) list and describe the main problems encountered in large classes;
 ii) list the main features of 'control' and 'independence' strategies for dealing with problems in large classes;
iii) describe and contrast different methods associated with these strategies.

This clearly provides much more information for the student than would a contents list or a syllabus listing. When they also provide a strong framework for assessment, objectives make it very explicit what is to to be learnt.

Behavioural objectives became very widely used in the USA in the fifties and sixties and are still the basis of much course design and, in particular, objective testing such as the use of multiple choice questions. Objectives were adopted by the Open University in the 1970s for distance learning, to clarify course goals in the absence of contact between teacher and student, and to guide the writing of CMAs (Computer Marked Assignments). Formal statements of objectives are still the central feature of course design in B/TEC (Business and Technical Education Council) courses provided all over the UK for vocational courses. B/TEC have their own typology of levels of objectives and link the proportion of each level of objectives to the level of the course and the types of assessment methods used. They are used to standardise courses and control quality

b) *Highly structured course*. The purpose of a particular section of a course can be clarified by its function in relation to other sections of the course. Courses can be designed with considerable attention to the prerequisite knowledge, knowledge required for subsequent sections, logical ordering of material, remedial attention necessary at each stage, and so on. A systematic approach to course design can lead to the kind of structure illustrated in Figure 3.1, designed to cope with students with a wide range of ability in English. This kind of approach to course design is most appropriate to subject matter which has its own logical structure involving clear sequences of prerequisites.

Problem 2: Lack of knowledge of progress

The control strategy involves testing students by asking questions to which the teacher has the correct answer, and informing students whether they are correct or not.

a) *Objective testing*. The most common form of objective testing is the multiple choice question test, although there are quite a range of possible formats of question which allow students to record their answers in a way which can be quickly and objectively marked (see Gibbs *et al*, 1988). The ease of marking allows frequent and extensive testing and the use of computers, either with optical mark readers (OMRs) or screen-based systems, increases the speed and ease still further. The installation of a computer-marking system at Oxford Polytechnic has led to a wide range of applications, within subjects such as education and economics as well as science and technology. Several of the chapters below describe courses which use objective testing to keep track of students progress and to feed back information to them about their progress.

b) *Programmed instruction and CAL*. Programmed instruction and its applications with computers involves learners working through a long series of very short tutorial steps. Each step involves some input of material followed by a test of of that material. Students are directed to the next step or to remedial material depending on their response. This is the ultimate

Figure 3.1 The instructional sequence of a freshman English course at Syracuse University.
Source: Rogers and Burnett (1980)

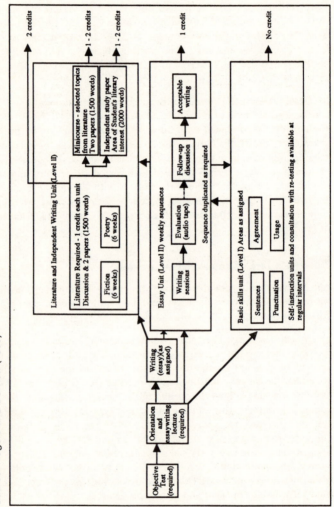

Essay Marking Criteria

Knowledge

Text	deep, thorough, detailed	☐☐☐☐☐	superficial
Author	wide knowledge used in analysis	☐☐☐☐☐	no knowledge or not used
Genre	wide knowledge used in analysis	☐☐☐☐☐	no knowledge or not used
Historial and social context	wide knowledge used in analysis	☐☐☐☐☐	no knowledge or not used

Essay

Structure	clear, logical structure	☐☐☐☐☐	confused list
Quotations	correct, purposeful use, properly referenced	☐☐☐☐☐	incorrect, arbitrary use
Other sources	wide range, relevant properly referenced	☐☐☐☐☐	few, irrelevant, improperly referenced
Grammar, spelling	correct	☐☐☐☐☐	poor

Personal Response to Text

Response	vivid, personal	☐☐☐☐☐	little response
Viewpoint	clearly expressed	☐☐☐☐☐	no viewpoint
Creativity	imaginative, surprising	☐☐☐☐☐	predictable

Critical Theory

Understanding	clear grasp	☐☐☐☐☐	little grasp
Use of methods	wide range, appropriate use	☐☐☐☐☐	little or inappropriate use

Figure 3.2 An assignment form for English Literature essays

level of control it is possible to exert over student learning – each minute step is under the control of the designer of the programme. More flexible types of tutorial programme have been developed for computer-assisted learning, and it has been greatly enlivened by colour, graphics, moving images, touch screens, sound and even interaction with video, audio or CD. However programmed learning remains a control strategy.

Problem 3: Lack of advice on improvement

The control strategy consists of mechanising feedback. It uses criteria, and sometimes even feedback, which are fixed to the course rather than responsive to the individual.

a) *Assignment attachment forms*. Assignment attachment forms are used by tutors to give structured feedback to students on their written work. They usually involve a list of criteria and rating scales and tutors tick boxes on the scales to give students feedback, as in Figure 3.2, an example from an English Literature course.

b) *Automated tutorial feedback*. Multiple choice question testing based on computers can have tutorial comments attached to each incorrect response so that students get back not just a print-out of their test score but a tutorial comment for each incorrect answer given. These tutorial comments are written at the same time as the tests. It is possible to use computer marked tests not to allocate marks but purely for feedback to students, and questions and their tutorial comments can be written with this feedback role in mind.

Problem 4: Inability to support reading

The control strategy consists of specifying set readings and providing these in full for all students.

a) *Use of set books*. Many undergraduate courses in North America, and most in the first year, use a set textbook. Use of textbooks can guarantee that students have access to core material but may also make it likely that they do not go far beyond this core material. Many textbooks come with sets of multiple choice test questions, study guides and tutor guides, so that whole courses can be built around them with little extra design work.

b) *Use of learning packages*. Learning packages can provide students with much of the reading material they need and refer them to any additional sources (Adams *et al* 1988). They may also include questions about the reading and short tasks. In elaborate forms they may resemble distance-learning materials such as Open University course units. In this form the packages often attempt to control minute details of students' learning from moment to moment by taking them through material in a logical step-by-step manner with questions and answers interspersed with the text.

Chapter Five describes the development and use of extensive learning packages in an introductory Law course.

Problem 5: Inability to support independent study

The control strategy consists of narrowing and controlling the range of student independent study through specifying purposes, activities, resources, steps to be taken etc. Such controlled study may consist of little more than following a series of instructions.

a) *Structured projects*. Appendix 3-A contains extracts from a Geography course where large numbers of students undertake project work. To reduce the need for frequent supervision by tutors detailed instructions are given on how to undertake the project. Without such instructions, and with the limited resources available, students might not have coped with the task.

b) *Lab guides*. Lab guides can contain all the instructions students need to undertake an experiment, use a piece of equipment or analyse results. Guides can contain diagrams of equipment, whole sections of lab reports ready written, data recording sheets, graphs with the axes already correctly labelled, and so on (see Jaques and Gibbs (1990) for examples). While it is possible to substitute for a considerable amount of the face-to-face support students would otherwise have obtained from tutors or demonstrators, lab guides may leave students with little to do but follow instructions. As a result such guides have become known as 'recipe books'. However it is possible to be selective about which aspects of the lab to provide detailed written support for, leaving students to focus on one aspect of the lab independently each week, for example the experimental design, setting up the equipment, error estimation or interpreting the data.

Problem 6: Lack of opportunity for discussion

The control strategy consists of introducing discussion of teacher-set questions and tasks in fixed time slots within teacher-directed sessions.

a) *Structured lectures.* Chapter Four by Alan Jenkins describes the use of active learning in lectures. In large lecture classes it is impossible to bring about open unstructured discussion but it is possible to introduce short discussion activities for pairs or threes. It requires very clear instructions, strict timekeeping and a firm hand regaining control in order to continue the lecture, but it can be done (Gibbs, 1992a). A considerable degree of control needs to be exerted to cope with very large numbers. Such discussions are inevitably limited in scope.

b) *Structured seminars/workshops.* As seminar groups grow to above ten or so, unstructured discussions become less satisfactory and the majority of students present will not participate to any great extent. However a wide range of structures can be used to encourage active participation, such as rounds, pyramids, line-ups, pairs, syndicates and brainstorming (Gibbs, 1992b). Pyramids, for example, involve students working on their own, then in pairs, then in fours, and finally as a whole class. By building up to open discussion in this way students develop their ideas and their confidence and are more likely to contribute productively even when the class is as large as 30.

All these methods, however effective at getting students to join in, involve control of the class and of the topics being discussed.

Problem 7: Inability to cope with variety of students

The control strategy consists of controlling entry and progress so that only those students who pass teacher-set tests can proceed. It is well suited to well structured curricula in mathematics and the sciences where prerequisite knowledge can be specified clearly.

a) *Pre-tests plus remedial material.* Highly structured courses with clear objectives often specify the level of knowledge or competence expected on entry. It is possible to set entry tests, or 'pre-tests' to check on students' prior knowledge. You can then either turn away unsuitable students, referring them to a more suitable lower-level course, or offer remedial material so that students can catch up in their own time in parallel with the course (as in

Figure 3.1). This remedial material can be computer-based or in independent learning packages in the library, and may make no demands on the tutors at all. Such remedial material would typically include self-tests so that students can check for themselves when they have reached an acceptable standard in relation to the entry level for the course.

b) *Self-paced study (PSI)*. This involves allowing students to progress as fast as they are able or as slow as they need. It usually requires clearly stated objectives and a course divided into self-contained units each with its own objectives and objective tests. In the 'Keller Plan' or 'Personalised System of Instruction' (PSI) students study independently and sit a test for a unit whenever they feel ready. If they pass the test they are given the objectives for the next unit. The main teaching comes when a student fails a test. Such approaches can be very cost-effective, being both economical and successful. Elements of this strategy can be found in Chapters Six and Seven, in that regular test results enable students to make appropriate decisions about which aspects of the teaching support to make use of.

Problem 8: Inability to motivate students

The control strategy relies on extrinsic motivation, usually centred on the desire to pass teacher-set tests, or at least on the desire to avoid failing such tests.

a) *Frequent testing*. The Modular Course at Oxford Polytechnic, with its one-term modules and extensive coursework assessment, involves more regular assessment than many institutions in the UK, and some modules use computer-marked tests regularly (see Chapters Six and Seven). This can lead to very strategic students who know exactly how well they are doing. Students can spend the bulk of their learning time on assessed tasks, with deadlines providing the main motivation.

b) *High failure rates*. In the UK imposed high failure rates are found largely on courses controlled by professions (the law, banking, accountancy) where pass rates may be as low as 50 per cent. The high chance of failing leads to compliant and hard-working students regardless of the quality of the teaching or inherent interest of the material or the learning tasks. Outside of externally controlled professional courses high failure rates are rare in the UK. They are very much more common in Europe and, to a lesser extent, North America. In the UK it is still largely the case that a high failure rate is seen as a failure of the course, rather than a failure of the students. However the power of high failure rates to control student behaviour is unlikely to go unexploited for long.

Independence strategies

Problem 1: Lack of clarity of purpose

Independence strategies involve students specifying their own purposes in personally relevant ways, or setting the tackling and solving of problems as the goal instead of more abstract specifications of learning outcomes.

a) *Use of learning contracts.* Learning contracts are agreements between teachers and students about learning. They can involve statements about what is to be learnt, what resources will be used, what steps will be taken in order to achieve the desired outcomes, what the outcomes will look like and how they will be assessed. They are normally negotiated between teachers and students in order to give a clear purpose to independent studying. Learning contracts can be very extensive, involving an entire qualification, (as at Suffolk College) or quite modest, involving a few days' work experience. Learning contracts can provide a framework within which students can supervise their own independent learning, confident in their goals.

b) *Problem-based learning.* Problem-based learning provides problems to be tackled, through which learning takes place. For the learner the purpose of the activity is clear even if the learning outcomes are not yet obvious. People seem to have a natural propensity to tackle problems and find them inherently engaging. In some forms of problem-based learning there is a detailed analysis of the knowledge base the problem draws upon, to guide learners, and most problem-based learning also involves groups who help to give direction to learning.

Problem 2: Lack of knowledge of progress

Independence strategies involve developing students' ability to recognise their own progress and judge their own work, even to the point of awarding themselves grades.

a) *Development of student judgement.* When tutors take all the responsibility for marking, students often hand in work for assessment without even reading it. They may have little idea what mark it might get or why. Academics do not rely entirely on others for a sense of the quality of their own work – they make their own judgements and re-draft and improve their own work. If students are to monitor their own performance and correct their own work they need to develop their criteria and judgement about what quality consists of in academic work. They need to undertake marking exercises, see other students' work, and discuss what is good and bad about a variety of assignments.

b) *Self-assessment.* One very effective way of developing students' judgement is to require them to write self-assessment comments on their own work before they submit it, on a self-assessment sheet. Such sheets can include questions such as the following:

• What are the best features of your assignment?

- How could your assignment be improved?
- What would you have to do to get one grade higher than the grade you are going to get?

Students need to develop a sense of when they have done enough on a topic and when they can move on to the next task – they need to assess their own progress and achievements.

Problem 3: Lack of advice on improvement

Independence strategies involve using students to give feedback to each other, either informally or through formal assessment processes.

a) *Peer feedback and assessment.* Students are perfectly capable of giving useful feedback on each other's work. Indeed it can be very effective to require students to obtain feedback on an essay or lab report, and to show how they have responded to this feedback in the final draft which is submitted for assessment. In technical areas it is easy to give students marking schemes to mark each other's work. Studies have shown that peers can be very reliable and monitoring for collusion is relatively straightforward (Boud, 1986). In some situations, such as in seminar work or group project work, peers are in the best position to give feedback and even to allocate marks, and a range of workable techniques exist to ensure fairness.

Problem 4: Inability to support reading

Independence strategies involve widening the range of relevant sources so that students are not all chasing the same material at once. This implies wider varieties of assignments and also the development of students' ability to locate and use a wider variety of information sources.

a) *Development of students' research skills.* In Chapter Ten a sociology course is described in which resources are allocated in the first term to enable students to develop the research skills necessary to cope with less support in the second and third terms. The course is supported by a workbook containing a series of library search exercises, some of which are assessed. Students reliant on textbooks and learning packages containing all the necessary reading can become dependent on such support and may not develop the necessary research skills. With library resources so stretched, students very often find that the recommended book is out. With research skills they can cope with this problem in a variety of ways.

b) *More varied assignments.* One way of getting round the problem of 200 students chasing the same sources is to invent more varied assignments which draw on a wider range of sources both within the library and outside. For example a Business Law programme at Wolverhampton Polytechnic involves teams of students going to business libraries, the Department of

Trade and Industry, and to a range of the kinds of information source which lawyers actually use. This requires more independence, of course, but with sufficient thought and support even first-year students need not be restricted in their reading.

Problem 5: Inability to support independent study

Independence strategies tend to involve the use of students to 'supervise' and support each other, through group projects and learning teams, and also the use of structures provided by learning contracts as a framework within which such support can be provided.

a) *Group work*. Students can tackle more complex, more extensive and more open-ended projects if they work in groups. Instead of relying on one-to-one supervision tutors need only supervise the group. And if attention is paid to developing group-work skills the group can become very effective at managing itself and supervising its members. Seminar groups can be set up to run independent tutorless seminar groups. Project teams can be set up to undertake independent field work and research. Laboratory groups can be set up to design, run and write up practical experimentation. Assessment methods are available to allocate marks to individuals within groups when the group submits a single product for assessment.

b) *Learning teams*. Chapter Nine describes how learning teams were set up on a large part-time BA Business Studies course to support the independent study of mature students. There had previously been very little contact with tutors but the learning teams provided peer tuition and support. Learning teams can share reading material and lecture notes, comment on each other's essays, provide 'personal tutoring', revise together and generally support each other's learning.

Problem 6: Lack of opportunity for discussion

Independence strategies make use of students' ability to hold discussions on their own, either through formal student-led seminars, or through co-operative work on assignments.

a) *Student-led seminars*. Students can run their own seminar groups without a tutor present. At Oxford Polytechnic, education students take turns, in pairs, to take responsibility for a seminar session. They give a presentation, provide handouts and follow-up references and lead a discussion. As they are assessed by the rest of their group they take this responsibility seriously and make sure the session is engaging and well run. Meanwhile a tutor is touring a number of parallel independent seminar groups to make sure they are OK. There isn't usually much work for the tutor to do (Gibbs, 1992b).

b) *Team assignments*. Students can learn to co-operate on assignments and projects, laboratory work, fieldwork, seminar presentations and even reading assignments. This can generate a great deal of discussion outside of class. The assessment requirements and the design of classroom sessions are powerful tools to influence the ways in which students study independently.

Problem 7: Inability to cope with variety of students

Independence strategies place the responsibility on students to make use of a range of opportunities to suit their own varying needs. They can also place value on the progress students make in their learning rather than on the particular place they end up at, so accepting differences in learning outcomes rather than seeing them as a problem to be avoided.

a) *Variety of support mechanisms*. Students can be offered optional self-check tests, remedial lectures, optional problem classes and surgeries, additional reading lists, optional self-help groups, access to additional video or computer-assisted learning material in the library and a whole host of optional extras. Different students with different learning styles and preferences, as well as different needs, will take advantage of these extras to different extents. One-to-one tutorial support would be too expensive to provide for everyone, but few actually take advantage of surgery slots that have to be signed up for so they can be provided quite cheaply. Similarly CAL software and micros might be prohibitively expensive to provide for all students but, as an option on open access in the library, would provide a valuable extra for those that chose to use it. The crucial element is student choice in taking advantage of opportunities.

b) *Negotiated goals*. Contract learning, in which learning goals are negotiated, allow students to set themselves and reach targets which are suitable for their level of experience and competence and also which match their aspirations. Students can negotiate for a contract which would get them a 'C' grade if completed successfully, or an 'A' grade if they are more ambitious. Different levels of support can be provided for students to enable them to achieve different objectives within the same course. Students always achieve different levels anyway and you can build this reality into your planning.

Problem 8: Inability to motivate students

Independence strategies focus on intrinsic motivation: on students being interested because they are pursuing interesting tasks and their own goals in their own ways.

a) *Engaging learning tasks*. This simply involves concentrating on devising learning tasks which are intrinsically engaging. This can involve open-ended extended project work, problem-based learning and interdisciplinary work rather than closed, short, routine, narrow and predictable tasks. Teaching should be designed to support engaging learning tasks rather than worrying about the teaching and forgetting what students are going to be doing on their own.

b) *Co-operative learning.* Much co-operative learning is highly engaging, whether it involves peer feedback, autonomous small group seminars, shared laboratory experiments, group project work or learning teams. If you can find ways of binding students together in co-operative action this will tend to be more motivating than leaving them to compete in isolation.

Using control and independence strategies together

In practice many courses, and most of our case studies, use a variety of methods which involve a mixture of control and independence strategies. For example, Chapter Seven describes the use of objectives and objective tests in a Physics course but uses the test results not for assessment purposes but to provide information for the students to use to make independent decisions about which of the support mechanisms they need to use to reach the set objectives. Chapter Eight describes fieldwork in geography which involves both highly structured field work exercises and the use of independent groups to undertake these exercises.

Strong elements of structure are often necessary in large classes to enable the operation of what might otherwise be unmanageable complexity and variety. And students like a clear framework within which they study. If things are too open-ended they will need more tutorial support, not less. But the control element here is generally one of process rather than content, as with the fieldwork case study.

Clear structure to content can also allow students to make more choices and exercise some independence. For example if a course is structured into a series of relatively self-contained units, each with its own objectives and sample test material, it can be possible for students to spend less time on those units they find they can handle and focus their attention on those units which will require more of their effort, as with Chapter Six. It requires the discipline and structure of a control strategy to provide students with sufficient information to exploit the flexibility available and foster this kind of independence.

Highly structured courses can benefit greatly from independence strategies for part of their operation. For example in the course described in Chapter Nine, the learning outcomes, and even the course syllabus listings, remained fixed by teachers and teaching was almost exclusively through mass lectures. Students had to achieve much the same level of knowledge in specified areas if they were to succeed in the subsequent second year of the course, and still took teacher-set end of year exams. But the use of 'Study Networks', involving learning teams added a major new dimension to an otherwise teacher-centred course, and enabled the course to cope with increased class size at the same time.

We know of a Public Health Medicine course where the syllabus and a list of competencies are specified in considerable detail, but where the ways these are 'covered' or achieved is negotiated between student and supervisor through a series of work-based learning contracts. There is considerable flexibility and independence which would have been hard to manage without the strong underlying structure. In fact, prior to the development of the list of competencies and the use of learning contracts, students' work had been much narrower, more predictable in nature, and more focussed around the supervisor's demands.

On some courses, however, the strategies are mixed in ways which do not work. Students appear to be asked to be independent, while in reality they have little scope for manoeuvre and are rewarded for conformity. They may be asked to draw up learning contracts but are then assessed by teachers using their own pre-set criteria. Students may be asked to work co-operatively in teams, but be set such predictable and pre-defined tasks that the group work is as controlled as if they were on their own following instructions. Students may be asked to be creative even where learning objectives are pre-specified and tests are tightly linked to these objectives. Students can be given conflicting messages about what the real task is and about what would count as acceptable performance on a course. The problem is usually that there is more control, and less scope for independence, than is claimed by teachers. Students' motivation and involvement soon suffers. Teachers complain that independence strategies don't work or that students are conservative in their study habits when the real problem is a confusion of strategies.

The case studies

The case studies which follow illustrate a wide range of strategies being pursued: from the Keller Plan biology course, in Chapter Six, which is at the control end of the spectrum, to the geography field work in Chapter Eight, which is towards the independence end of the spectrum. There are more examples of control strategies here, perhaps because independence strategies are normally associated with resource-intensive tutorial support. In time perhaps we will find more examples of economical independent learning which exploits the potential of the methods described above.

Some of the changes described involve innovations which do not employ either of these strategies. For example the differences between 'cheap' and 'expensive' second-year sociology courses in Chapter Ten are largely differences in quantity of seminars and coursework within a completely conventional course delivery model: saving resources in one course in order to be able to spend them in another course. This is a resource strategy rather than an educational strategy. We would argue, however, that retaining quality must involve decisions not just about the quantity of teaching and assessment students are provided with, but the overall educational strategy for providing it. Conventional approaches offer little long-term protection for quality and either control or independence strategies need to be adopted in a deliberate way. We hope that the case studies illustrate purposeful decision making and strategic approaches to retaining quality in large classes.

References

Adams, D., Gibbs, G., Jaques, D. and Watson, D. (1988) *Workbooks: a Practical Guide*. Oxford Polytechnic: Educational Methods Unit.

Boud, D. (1986) *Implementing Student Self-Assessment*, Herdsa Green Guide No 5, Sydney: Higher Education Research and Development Society of Australia.

Gibbs, G. (1992a) *Lecturing To More Students*. No 2 in the series Teaching More Students. Oxford: Oxford Centre for Staff Development.

Gibbs, G. (1992b) *Discussion With More Students*. No 3 in the series Teaching More Students. Oxford Polytechnic: Oxford Centre for Staff Development.

Gibbs, G., Habeshaw, S. and Habeshaw, T. (1988) *53 Interesting Ways To Assess Your Students* Bristol: TES.

Jaques, D. and Gibbs, G. (1990) *Labs and Practicals*. Oxford Polytechnic: Educational Methods Unit.

Jenkins, A. and Pepper D. (1989) *Enhancing Employability and Educational Experience*. SCED Paper 27. Birmingham: SCED.

Rogers, C. A. and Burnett, R. E. (1980) *Student Manuals. Their Rationale and Design*. University of Syracuse: Center for Instructional Development.

Further reading on control and independence strategies

Control strategies

Setting objectives
Bloom, B. (1964) *Taxonomy of Educational Objectives*. Vols. 1 and 2. Longman.

Objective testing
Gronlund, N. E. (1988) *How to construct achievement tests.* New Jersey: Prentice-Hall.

Ward, C. (1981) *Preparing and using objective questions.* Cheltenham: Stanley Thomas.

Course guides and workbooks
Adams, D., Gibbs, G., Jaques, D. and Watson, D. (1988) *Workbooks: a Practical Guide*. Oxford Polytechnic: Educational Methods Unit.

Rogers, C. A. and Burnett, R. E. (1980) *Student Manuals. Their Rationale and Design*. University of Syracuse: Center for Instructional Development.

Rowntree, D. (1990) *Teaching through self-instruction.* London: Kogan Page.

Computers in assessment
Brohn, D. M. (1986) 'The use of computers in assessment in higher education', *Assessment and Evaluation in Higher Education*, 11 (3), 231–9.

Gibbs, G. ed (1985) *Objective tests and computer applications.* SCED Paper 21 Birmingham Polytechnic: SCED.

Gibbs, G. (1987) *Using the Optical Mark Reader: 2. Multiple Choice Question Tests*. Oxford Polytechnic: Educational Methods Unit.

Individualised instruction (including Keller Plan)
Boud, D. (1985) 'Individualised Instruction in Higher Education', In T. Husen and T. N. Postlethwaite eds *International Encyclopaedia of Education: Research and Studies*, 5, pp 2451-7. Oxford: Pergamon.

Goldschmid, B. and Goldschmid, M. L. (1974) 'Individualising Instruction in Higher Education: a Review', *Higher Education*, 3, 1-24.

Runquist, O. (1979) 'Programmed independent study, laboratory technique course for general chemistry', *Journal of Chemical Education*, 56, 616-7.

Computer Assisted Learning (CAL and CBL)
O'Shea, T. and Self, J. (1983) *Learning and teaching with computers*. Brighton: Harvester Press.

Assignment attachment forms
McDonald, R. and Murray, B. (1985) 'Use of assignment attachments in assessment', *Assessment in Higher Education*, 5 (1), 45-55.

Structured projects
Jenkins, A. and Pepper, D. (1989) *Enhancing Employability and Educational Experience*. SCED Paper 27. Birmingham: SCED.

Independence strategies

Use of learning contracts
Knowles, M. S. (1986) *On Using Learning Contracts*. San Francisco: Jossey Bass.

Tomkins, C. and McGraw, M. (1988) 'The negotiated learning contract' in D. Boud ed op cit 172-91.

Problem-based learning
Boud, D. and Felletti, G. eds (1991) *The Challenge of Problem-based Learning*. London: Kogan Page.

Self and peer assessment
Boud, D. (1986) *Implementing student self-assessment* Herdsa Green Guide No. 5. Sydney: Higher Education Research and Development Society of Australia.

Brown S. and Dove, P. eds (1991) *Self and peer assessment*. SCED Paper 63. Birmingham: SCED.

Development of independence and learning skills
Boud, D. (1988) *Developing Student Autonomy in Learning*. (2nd edn) London: Kogan Page.

Habeshaw, T., Habeshaw, S. and Gibbs, G. (1989) *53 Interesting Ways To Help Your Students To Study*. Bristol: TES.

More varied assignments
Gibbs, G. Habeshaw, S. and Habeshaw, T. (1988) *53 Interesting Ways To Assess Your Students*. Bristol: TES.

Rowntree, D. (1987) *Assessing students: how shall we know them?* London: Kogan Page.

Independent Groups
Collier, K. G. ed (1983) *The management of peer group learning.* Guildford: SRHE.
Goodlad, S. (1989) *Peer tutoring.* London: Kogan Page.
Jaques, D. (1991) *Learning in Groups.* London: Kogan Page.

Appendix 3-A

Structured project and group work in geography

The example here is a simulation exercise: 'Role Playing Royal Commission', designed by John Gold and is extracted from Jenkins and Pepper 1989.

Brief description

The class takes on the form of a Royal Commission. Students are briefed to represent the viewpoints of various interest groups over a period of weeks.

What the teacher does

Decide upon the issue to be investigated. This approach is particularly suitable for analysing how different interest groups formulate their courses of action on the same issue. Thus it is suited to a wide variety of political or social issues which in the 'real world' could be the subject of a Royal Commission (or Public Inquiry) – see the description of an inquiry into the problems of the inner city. The method can also be used for issues of a more overtly scientific nature eg what are the the best forms of sea defences or what are the causes of and solutions to the problems of acid rain?

Decide upon the interest groups to be represented at the inquiry. The number of interest groups will largely depend on the variety of interest groups and opinions on this issue in the 'real world' and the number of students for whom you have to find roles. Each interest group should be formed of about two to four people: if a group becomes larger than four, co-ordinating it can become difficult and some students may play a very marginal role.

Pick one student to chair the Royal Commission. This should not be left to student choice. Much of the success of the exercise depends upon the person playing this role. They needs to be someone liked and respected by their peers but able to act in authority. Of course you (or another member of staff) can choose to play that role but it then becomes a teacher-centred rather than a student-centred activity.

Divide students into the various interest groups in whatever way you think appropriate. It can be very valuable for students to take on a role with which they are initially not in sympathy. This can enable them to get to grips with a viewpoint they do not readily understand. However this presents a danger that they will not forcibly or convincingly argue from that position.

Extracts from student handouts outlining Royal Commission procedures

Assignment: 'Royal Commission on the Problems of the Inner City'

By decree of 'Parliament', a 'Royal Commission' has been established to investigate the state of government policy towards the inner city. Its terms of reference are:

to investigate the problems of the inner city, to discover the nature of those problems, their causes and their consequences, and to make recommendations about the priorities that should be adopted in future planning for the inner city.

The Commission has decided to supplement its own readings of documentation and other literature by calling evidence from the following bodies:

- The City of Birmingham
- The City of Glasgow
- The Confederation of British Industry
- The Trades Union Congress
- The Church of England
- The Town and Country Planning Association

You can play either of two roles:

1. Represent one of these interest groups both in the form of a written submission (to be written as a group paper) and by speaking and acting on behalf of your interest group in all the class sessions.
2. Act as a member of the Commission, whereby you will hear evidence, cross-question your witnesses, sift through the evidence and prepare a joint report.

In either case, 50 per cent of the marks for this assignment are awarded for the written paper supplied by your group and 50 per cent for your own group's performance in the class sessions, ie how convincingly you have performed your role. Remember, if you are to represent an interest group satisfactorily, you must be prepared to twist the evidence, lie convincingly and do whatever else is necessary to support your case – just as you would if this was a real Commission of Inquiry. The success of any simulation depends on the willingness of all participants to enter into the spirit of the exercise. This criterion will be taken into account in marking the simulation.

You are free to take on any role that you wish, subject to the fact that Parliament, in the shape of your tutor, will be appointing the Chairperson.

TIMETABLE (2-hour session each week)

Week	Tasks
1	Introductory session (Teacher), followed by brief plenary session.
2	Evidence from (1) City of Birmingham (2) City of Glasgow.
3	Evidence from (1) CBI (2) TUC.
4	Evidence from (1) Church of England (2) TCPA.
4–8	Commission prepares report, which is handed in for duplication and distribution.
9	Beginning of week – pick up copy of report for reading before the last session.
Final Session	Commission presents report, cross-examination of Commission, de-briefing.

Chapter 4

Active learning in structured lectures

Alan Jenkins

SUMMARY

Some of the methods of course delivery outlined in Chapter Three require teachers to adopt totally new ways of delivering courses . Alternatively one can innovate and hold on to quality by gradually changing traditional methods. In the traditional lecture teachers speak with little or no interruption for some 50 minutes. This case study shows how by breaking up the lecture into short segments, many of which are devoted to students in small groups working at tasks devised by the lecturer, students in large classes can work actively and feel personally involved. This method requires teachers to learn new skills, particularly how to design and manage tasks. However, one can adopt the method in stages starting by including a short break into a conventional lecture.

I was shocked at first that I had to participate in group discussions rather than the usual sit-at-the-back-and-fall-asleep syndrome

A classroom described

Picture a classroom in which some 100 students are sitting. The room is oblong in shape, flat floored with chairs and tables that can easily be moved. At the front of the room there is a an overhead projector and a large scale video screen. At the beginning of the session students arrange themselves and the furniture so they can sit and work in groups of two or three. Knowing that is the custom of the class, they each pick up a six to ten page handout which sets out the structure of the session, with space for them to take notes. It contains extracts from texts and newspaper articles. All students should have the course textbook on their desks. At the beginning of the class, the teacher (myself) talks to the students from the front of the class recalling what they did last week and setting up this week's theme. This is aided by showing a short segment from a recent television documentary programme. But soon I stop talking to the class as a whole. Students are set a task to do – to discuss an aspect of the television programme or to read an extract from the course text or part of this week's handout. They are directed to consider specific issues. They know they are expected to discuss and work at these in their small groups.

After groups have worked on a task I go over parts of it, clarifying where I judge that they have had difficulty but also pointing out complexities or introducing further ideas. If I think it appropriate, particularly if I want to convey a structured set of ideas or perhaps to convey information, I will speak (lecture) for up to ten or so minutes. But such lecturettes are limited. Much (and sometimes most) of the class time is for students to work on tasks. Table 4.1 describes one such class where I am teaching a theory which seeks to explain the location of towns (Christaller's central place theory). The 60 minute class contained 13 different sections; 6 periods of teacher talk (totalling 32 minutes) and 7 periods of student activity (totalling 25 minutes). The longest period of lecturer talk was 9 minutes and the longest period of student work was 6 minutes. Though the class I have in my mind is a first-term first-year Human Geography course, its basic principles can be applied to large classes in any discipline where the teacher wishes to encourage active learning. I will call this method 'structured lectures' in contrast to the 'conventional lecture' in which the teacher talks uninterrupted generally for 50 or 60 minutes.

Origins and rationale

There is nothing particularly new in this method of teaching. Many of its basic features I obtained from Donald Bligh's now classic *What's the Use of Lectures?* (1972). What I contribute here is over 15 years' experience in applying and developing the method at first in classes of about 50 students and then in classes of 80 to 120, at first in the conventional one hour teaching slot and lately in a three hour slot. Also for one year, while teaching in the USA I tried to adapt the method to teaching some 600 students in an introductory 100 level course.

What led me to the method was a dissatisfaction with the conventional lecture. Drawing on a variety of research studies Bligh convincingly demonstrates the limitations of the conventional lecture: 'Comparisons of the lecture method with other teaching methods . . . suggests that it . . . cannot be used on its own to promote thought or to change and develop attitudes without variations in the usual lecture techniques' (Bligh, 1972, 13).

It is important to restate briefly some of the basic limitations of the conventional lecture, whatever the class size to which it is addressed. I will then argue that lecturing to large groups poses further problems and then set out the rationale of the alternative structured method which is analysed here.

There are two major problems with conventional lectures. One is that

Stage	Activity	Time
1	A revision OHP transparency is displayed, summarising previous work related to the topic of the lecture. This uses time, normally wasted as students roll in, to wind up students' existing knowledge, ready to help them to make sense of new concepts which will be presented.	5 mins
2	Revision talk on the previous lecture, involving a transparency summary and printed handouts. This pulls together relevant material covered in earlier parts of the course which provide a background to the new material.	9 mins
3	Student task: The question *What aspects of central place theory can be used to analyse the number and location of shopping facilities in towns?* was displayed. Students are asked to discuss the question in twos or threes. The lecturer wanders amongst students, listening and helping, clarifying the task where necessary.	5 mins
4	The lecturer gives a short lecture, answering the question and introducing new material. Students add their own points to handouts.	7 mins
5	Students are set a new task to discuss in paris, involving applying the new theoretical concepts to some data presented on the screen. The lecturer moves amongst the students to see if they have got the hang of it. As soon as he is satisfied . . .	4 mins
6	. . . the lecturer summarises some of the students' answers, and comments and gives feedback on the students' learning. This is followed by a three minute lecture developing the concepts further.	6 mins
7	Students are then set a harder task involving interpreting changes over time in the location of towns, presented on four simplified maps. The task is to explain the changes using the theory. Students work in pairs. There is a buzz of activity at a point in the lecture where there is usually a trough of attention.	6 mins
8	The lecturer answers part of the question, and leads students into a more advanced issue.	1 min
9	Students work on in their small groups.	2 mins
10	The lecturer completes the analysis of the maps and moves on to apply the concepts to various other situations in a short lecture.	3 mins
11	The class is set an open question, which involves applying the theory to a completely new context. Not enough time is allowed.	1 min
12	The lecturer goes over material in the handout which has not been discussed so far.	6 mins
13	Students are asked to write a brief summary of the lecture.	2 mins

Table 4.1 Time and motion analysis of a structured lecture

generally attention and student learning deteriorate markedly over the first 20 minutes or so. The second is that higher level educational goals which involve understanding, the application and evaluation of ideas, and so on, and which go beyond recall and description, cannot be easily achieved when students are largely passive, as they are during a conventional lecture. (See Bligh, 1972, Gibbs, 1982 and McKeachie, 1986 for summaries and discussion of the research evidence on the lecture method.)

Measures of student attention and arousal tend to show that after the first few minutes or so these deteriorate markedly. After about 20 minutes student performance bottoms out and remains at a low level until towards the end when it briefly and slightly rises. Evidently, this is a general pattern and may vary depending on subject matter, skill of the lecturer and so on. But studies of student note taking and tests soon after the lecture which require students to recall the information demonstrate this general pattern. Furthermore tests a few weeks or even days after the lecture often show decline in the information learned unless students are given in the class or soon after a task requiring them to apply that knowledge.

But as academics our objectives go beyond getting students to recall factual information. We want them to understand that information, to apply it, to think about its essential ideas, to relate its key concepts to others. Research evidence is pretty conclusive that the conventional lecture is not very effective at enabling students to achieve these higher level goals. As McKeachie (1986, 69) states:

> When measures of knowledge are used, the lecture tends to be as efficient as other methods. Alternatively, in those experiments involving measures of retention of information after the end of a course, measures of transfer of knowledge to new situations, or measures of problem solving, thinking, or attitude change, or motivation for further learning, the results tend to show differences favouring discussion methods over lecture.

The reasons for the limitations of the conventional lecture in not facilitating these higher level goals are not hard to find. Significant learning requires the learner to be active. Put crudely the only person who has to be active in a conventional lecture is the lecturer! A study of student thought processes during conventional lectures found that students were attempting to solve problems and to synthesise information for 1 per cent of the time, compared with 60 per cent of the time spent in passive and irrelevant thoughts (Bloom, 1953). Much student time can be spent taking notes without necessarily remembering or understanding the information. If we want students to learn new information we need to give them time to think about it and relate it to previous knowledge. To better ensure it is remembered and made part of them we need to give them tasks and problems to apply it. New ideas need to be 'negotiated' particularly through discussion. The one-way flow of the conventional lecture places far too many potential demands on students – to listen to information, to note down what they consider to be important, to relate it to previous knowledge. It is not surprising that most can only attain low level recording of information.

Faced with this research evidence, which my own experience as teacher and student confirms, most of my teaching is through individual and group projects, discussion of assigned reading, simulations, student presentations, debates etc, ie methods where the emphasis is on student activity and involvement (Jenkins and Pepper 1988 and 1989). It is quite usual for my courses to have no lectures, conventional or structured.

However these courses have relatively 'low' enrolments of 20–30 students where with careful allotment of my time I can supervise individual/group projects, organise students giving presentations etc. Such methods are much harder (perhaps impossible) to use in a large class, particularly where, for reasons of efficiency, one lecturer is mainly responsible.

This was the situation I was faced with; I had the responsibility of organising and doing most of the teaching on the term one, year one introductory Geography course and in my 15 years at the Polytechnic, the numbers enrolled had increased from 50 to 100 or 120.

Linking efficiency and effectiveness

Faced with these circumstances I decided that the lecture method had definite advantages. In particular, one lecturer can teach many students. Providing a room large enough can be found, the lecture method easily accommodates increased class enrolments. Furthermore, the lecture is a method readily understood by both staff and students. A large lecture class also provides that sense of theatre that some teachers (myself included) enjoy.

However, having decided for reasons of 'efficiency' to lecture, for reasons of 'effectiveness' I had to teach in a way that recognised and sought to overcome the limitations of the conventional lecture. I also had to find ways of helping students with the particular problems of being in a large class (see Chapters Two and Three). Recalling their experience of walking into a large class, students have commented that they found it 'daunting', being 'an individual lost in a theatre crowd' or a 'number at the end of the computer print-out'. A feeling of anonymity is compounded by not being able to ask questions. For even if the lecturer encourages students to ask questions (and for reasons of control one may not), for a student to ask a question in a large class can be intimidating. Relatedly it is very difficult for the student to get any feedback on how they are progressing. It is thus, in attempting to teach in a way that is both 'efficient' and 'effective' that I have developed the structured lecture.

I see such structured lectures as combining certain of the advantages of lectures and discussion-based methods. They enable students to achieve many of the more high level goals associated with discussion-based methods; for much of the class time is given over to small group discussion and problem solving. Structured lectures also have the advantages of the conventional lecture in capitalising on the ability of some lecturers to convey enthusiasm with subject matter, to provide a guide to reading and course assignments. In particular they capitalise on the efficiency of the lecture. Many discussion-based methods typically require a high ratio of staff to students. The structured lecture can (as can the conventional lecture) effectively teach relatively large numbers of students.

Having given a snapshot description of the method and explained the rationale for my adopting it, I will now analyse how I teach this way as a guide to others considering adopting it. I have regularly evaluated the method and the result of the evaluations will be incorporated into the discussion. The overwhelming student reaction to the method is very positive. However the method is not presented as a panacea – rather I will show that it has certain limitations and may not be appropriate in certain classes. In particular in a very large class it is more difficult, perhaps impossible, to stimulate the degree of interaction and discussion required to ensure active learning.

The method outlined

The central aspect is my view of the role or purpose of the lecture. A conventional lecture often attempts to convey a lot of information to students. Indeed when I describe the method to colleagues a frequent reaction is: 'How do you cover the material?' It has to be emphasised that in a structured lecture very little time or intention is given to conveying information. Rather my view is that valuable classroom time (and in particular my time) should not be spent on such a low level goal. Rather my and the students time together should be spent on higher level goals of analysis, synthesis etc. I do wish students to learn some information but this is often conveyed to them in lecture handouts, while I use the best available (and cheapest) textbook (and multiple copies of key articles) as the main way of covering the material.

The success of the method very much depends on students appreciating the purpose of the class. As this is a first-year course most were recently at high school. Culturally they expect me to tell them things to learn. In the first class of the course students are told as they enter to sit in groups of two or three and rearrange the furniture. They are then shown a graph representing the plunging attention and performance of students in a conventional lecture and asked to discuss in their groups what it means. I then explain why I will teach the course in this way and set out certain 'ground rules', eg that as they come in they should rearrange the furniture from the previous class, pick up a lecture handout, and by next class all have the course textbook. Furthermore, in the first class they are given a full course guide with details of assignments etc, the first two pages of which are given over to an explanation of the method and how they are expected to learn. I take great care to ensure that the first two classes require them to be very active. Video recordings of students in these classes show that even though some are first bemused and perhaps embarrassed by having to talk to strangers they quickly adapt. Though generally I give them 'freedom' who to sit by, that will vary depending upon when they were let out of their previous class. By week three of the course, they form pretty definite groups.

I also ensure that in the first few classes the ground rules and my expectations are re-emphasised and expanded. Thus, in the second and third classes I give great emphasis to how the textbook is to be used. Short sections will be read and analysed in class to get students into the author's approach and I will emphasise the textbook's role in the course.

Great care has to be taken in constructing the tasks and topics for students to discuss. These student comments indicate certain critical problems;

I think the idea of stopping for discussion is a good idea in principle although if you don't have a clue of the answer it was dead boring.

I often found the breaks for discussion often led to general chat: a nice break but not much help.

Half the time I wasn't clear what was wanted, and so spent the time trying to avoid the lecturer in his tours of the lecture theatre.

The central problems are in devising tasks that set students clear demands but which require them to work to get the answers. Some forms of questions and tasks seem much better than others at getting and maintaining interest and involvement. Basically students need to see a way of getting to grips with the problem without being able to get the right answer too quickly. In fact closed questions (to which there are clearly right and wrong answers) may seldom be useful. But open questions can lead to confusion and stuckness if they don't see what is required or how to tackle the problem. Large open-ended tasks seldom get the attention of students working alone, although they may be very suitable for small groups to work at. In devising tasks my experience suggests it is best to:

1. Make tasks and questions small enough to be conceptualised and tackled. Use a series of small tasks rather than one big one.
2. Use concrete examples, specific situations and contexts with which students are familiar, rather than abstract, general and unfamiliar problems.
3. If it is a large, and potentially difficult problem, then specify the steps that should be used in tackling it.
4. Do not put students into groups too early if the task requires step-by-step work. Once in groups, work in clearly specified steps does not get the attention it requires. Anyway, students can work on these tasks by themselves. They can then compare their answers.

TEACHER TALK

Last week we analysed an article from the <u>Observer</u> newspaper (Jan 4th.1987) that argued that 'Britain is becoming two nations - the North increasingly unemployed and the South benefiting from new service jobs'. Now we are going to consider a contrasting view of Britain's changing geography. Your handout reprints the article and gives you questions to consider. Read it and jot down some notes answering the questions. Do this first by yourselves. Later you will share your answers with your neighbours.

CLASSROOM HANDOUT

Read the attached leading article from the <u>Sunday Times </u>of the 4th January 1987
'The Nonsense of North - South'.
Why does the writer argue that:
(a) the generalisation of a North - South divide 'obscures more than it illumines' and that it is 'mythical'.
(b) 'the real economic inequality in Britain is...a rather more complicated division'.
(c) note any key phrases the journalist uses to strengthen her argument. Would this sort of wording be acceptable? a ' good idea' in academic writing? Why ?

TEACHER TALK

Now that you have considered your own answers to these questions, get into your groups of 2 - 3. Appoint one of you to chair and discuss your answer to these questions concentrating on question (c).

Figure 4.1 A task defined

5. Do not leave students alone too long when they are working on open-ended tasks. Get them to compare their answers at an early stage.
6. It is important to vary the type of task. It is very easy to fall in the trap of asking very repetitive style questions.
7. Make very clear demands for the *outcome* of work eg 'list five reasons why transport costs are not a simple function of distance', rather than 'discuss the relationship between transport costs and distance'.

Figure 4.1 provides an example of how I instruct students on one set of linked tasks. Over the years I have become more skilful at setting the tasks and judging how long students need to work on them. These are the central skills the teacher needs to develop. I am still working on them.

Graham Gibbs recently observed such a session and commented that at times in speaking to explain the written task instructions I slightly changed the task to the students' confusion. At other times, possibly fearing that some students had misinterpreted the task, I interrupted the groups when they were working (and student evaluations pick that out as a problem). I now try to ensure that the spoken instructions are brief and are also clearly stated in lecture handout and/or overhead transparency. I then shut up and let them get on with it. I am also experimenting by stating with every task I set:

- **Why** I want them to do it.
- **What** (precisely) they are to do.
- **When** it has to be completed by.
- **How** they are to do it (eg appoint a chair, brainstorm some possible answers and then agree on the three strongest explanations).

I am finding participants quickly get used to this way of working – though judging the time that different groups will need to complete the task is difficult. Here it is useful to include some questions that could be discussed (by more able students) at length. As students work on these tasks I move between the groups listening in to hear how they are coping. Approaching a group I will get close enough to hear but far enough away so I am not part of the group. If staying to listen in I am likely to sit crouched so I am unlikely to be at their eye level and where I can overhear two or three groups. Students can invite me in (but I might decline) while I am likely to join in some groups' discussions – particularly if I think they are having difficulty with the task or have easily completed it and need prompting to go further. In moving around the groups I will try not to be too predictable in my movements while at the same time systematically listening and if necessary helping as many groups as possible. If I consider I need to make a brief comment to the class as a whole, I am likely to speak from wherever I am standing. However when I want to talk for more than about a minute then I will move to the front of the class.

Learning as the teacher how to follow up a task is difficult. Here are comments from two students in the same class: 'People became aware that the breaks would last only a few minutes and that Alan Jenkins would answer the questions anyway'; another student commented: 'The lecturer kept on asking questions but very often did not answer them anyway.' After a period of student discussion I will often go over the tasks, highlighting key issues and clearing up areas of difficulty. But at other times I will purposefully not speak to the whole group about a task. This is designed to 'encourage' those who would otherwise sit back and wait for the answers. Even in a large class I am trying to set up a culture in which students take on much of the responsibility for their learning.

One area where I try to guide them towards autonomy is making notes which reflect their understanding of the class themes. Conventional lectures often implicitly emphasise note taking. Much student time and attention is given over to taking notes. There is research evidence that this can be a relatively passive activity with student devoting little thought to understanding and applying the class themes. After the class the notes are filed away as they go off to another class. Too often when the students attempt to use the notes for revision they make limited sense. I have experimented with giving students a full set of printed notes at the beginning of the class but decided this was inappropriate as it was not requiring them to be active. The approach to note taking in this course reflects the views of Howe and Godfrey (1978). They suggest that handouts with gaps and omissions help to maintain student attention and allow the production of a personalised set of notes without burdening them with spending much time passively taking notes. As one student commented: 'I feel the provision of skeletal notes to be filled out/understood as the session progresses . . . allows the student to concentrate . . . without having to worry about taking masses of notes and thus missing key points of the lecture.'

The printed handout which students pick up at the beginning of the class contains an outline of the structure for the session with space for extra notes to be added. Many of the tasks and discussion questions for groups to work on are in the handout. Students quickly get used to making notes that record their answers and their discussions. I always ensure that at or near the end of a session there will be a question or activity that requires students to write something that pulls together what they have learned from the session. If I want them to know or use certain factual information or to convey some detailed or complicated information then this will be included in the handout. This ensures that valuable student time is available for discussion. Over the years of developing this method I have come to see that getting students to write in class can significantly aid their learning, when that writing involves them processing and developing their own understanding. This is very different from writing down to note what the teacher states.

Though students quickly get used to this form of note taking, mid-term evaluations invariably indicate that for some there is a major problem. Here are two student comments:

> He never actually gets to the point. I want hard facts to revise from and not just scratchy notes.

> I want some hard facts to be able to look back at – not just a few notes I have made myself and may be completely wrong for all I know. With the exam in a few weeks' time I want a good set of notes to revise from.

Each year I get similar comments from a few students. My main response is to re-emphasise certain ground rules which I established at the beginning of the course. I read out again a section from the course guide. This will have been emphasised in the first two sessions, but with the exam approaching it has greater meaning:

> You will not get many detailed notes/much factual information from the plenary sessions (lectures). Such information is very important but I think you get that better by reading. In particular you are assumed/

required to be obtaining that information from the textbook. *The examination will test whether you have gained this factual information.*

Essentially my view is that it takes time for students to adapt to this style of teaching. Most have just completed high school exams (A-levels) in which there is much emphasis on remembering factual information. Even in small high school classes many were taught by the conventional lecture even with dictated notes.

So in responding to the evaluation I try to reassure them by saying that it will take time to learn this way, while making clear that is the way the course will be taught. I also use these comments to emphasise two features of the course which takes this analysis outside the structured lecture. Alongside the lecture, students in groups of 10 to 15 have a weekly seminar with a member of staff. The emphasis here is mainly on the development of certain key skills – using the library, speaking, working in groups and writing – but applied to the course themes. The final and main assignment for their seminar leader is an exercise which requires students to integrate certain of the central themes from the structured lectures with the more clearly factual material from the course textbook. So in responding to the mid-course evaluation I emphasise that the assessment criteria do require them to use factual information – but the emphasis is on their ability to analyse, discuss and structure that information.

Relatedly at this stage in the course I remind them of the form of the exam. This is a seen exam where a linked set of essay questions are given them a few days before the 'exam'. In the exam room they are not allowed to use books or notes. The questions require students to remember and use a certain amount of factual information but the question is posed so the emphasis is on analysis. Indeed the students are told that a central reason I use a seen exam is so they appreciate that knowing 'facts' is a necessary but not very important part of the course. They have actively to construct their understanding of the course.

For other teachers this discussion of factual information emphasises that some students will initially have difficulties with learning in structured lectures. One needs to give them space to talk through with each other and raise with you the difficulties they are facing. Teachers also have to ensure that the assessment system clearly reflects the higher level goals of discussion style classes.

A final area of difficulty is whether to allow/encourage students to ask questions. Clearly this can help their learning. However as class size increases individual students' questions can be difficult to hear, and their question may be of no interest to most students. So I now have two related ground rules: (1) I will not accept questions when I am speaking to the whole class, and (2) I will provide space in the class session to answer your questions and listen to your comments.

As I walk around and listen in to student discussions they can invite me in and they are encouraged to put their hands up if they need help. Occasionally in a session I will invite all groups to put written questions to me, eg 'having read the instructions to assignment three, state two questions you want me to answer so you are certain what is expected of you'. While they are working on a task, watching a film clip, etc, I will pick out what seem the key questions and then answer them.

Finding ways to respond in class to student queries is valuable to students. It is also essential to the effective use of my time. Because of commitments to research etc, I am only available to students at specific office hours. I want to reserve these for students on advanced courses carrying out more complex assignments and students in great difficulty. Thus in this large course I try to ensure that student queries are answered in class time.

Overwhelmingly positive

Aspects of students' evaluations of the method have already been built into this account. However, there is perhaps a danger I have presented a too negative picture and have frightened off those of you who might be willing to try it. That is not what I have tried to do! Rather, I have tried to emphasise the practical issues and problems one has to think through in implementing the method. It is important to emphasise that by the end of the course the predominant student reaction is very positive. Typical comments are:

> I was shocked at first that I had to participate in group discussions rather than the usual sit-at-the-back-of-the-class-and-fall-asleep syndrome.

> I liked the way we were able to stop and discuss questions with a neighbour. It helped you understand more and prevented you getting bored.

> I think discussions in the lectures is a good idea. It makes sure you are listening and aware of the points to which the lecturer is moving.

Colleagues who come into the class comment on the atmosphere being relaxed, even friendly, but purposeful. Students often say how they like working with their colleagues and that they can ask them and me for help.

Key developments and certain limitations

Over the years of using the method the key change has been my grov ing sense of how to teach this way – and that is what is reported here. In addition, three other key developments have shown me factors affecting the success and the limitations of the method. These factors are moving from a lecture theatre to a flat-floored room, the lecture timetable changed from two one-hour slots per week to a three-hour slot and attempting to teach some 600 students using the method.

When I started teaching a large class this way it was in a conventional lecture theatre. As this is the normal large classroom in many institutions it is important to emphasise that I found that the method worked quite effectively in such a room. I had to be very firm in insisting that students could only sit in groups of two or three to talk along a row – in groups of four they could not easily talk to each other (see Gibbs *et al*, 1984, 127 for suggestions on how to form groups of three or four in a tiered lecture theatre). I found that by walking up the aisles and along the rows I could get at many of the groups, though this was not ideal as there were some groups I could not readily reach. Indeed I felt that some students purposefully avoided me – and educationally I felt that to be their disadvantage!

I do see that one of the factors affecting the success of the method with the mass of students is the teacher's ability to get around and into the groups and this was a central reason why I obtained a large flat room with flexible furniture in which to teach. Though I have no hard evidence I think this has significantly improved the success of the class. However I would have no hesitation about using the method in a lecture theatre.

Much of my early experience with structured lectures was in the conventional 60 minute teaching slot and here I felt it was very effective. Lately the college moved to a three-hour slot and I certainly prefer teaching smaller upper-level courses that way. However I found it less easy to adapt the structured lecture to that length of time. A frequent student comment was that 'three hours is too long'. I experimented with various formats. A basic one was to take a half-hour break midway through the class. I tried to make the second session very different from the first, eg by showing and analysing a film, stopping the film every so often to get the groups to analyse it.

Towards the end of the term, as students got more comfortable with their role – and also, as in their seminar groups they had been working in a fixed group of four people to prepare a spoken presentation – in the second half of the three-hour slot, I got students to rearrange themselves and the furniture to sit in circles of four. I found that I could give these groups quite long and complicated tasks eg analysing an article guided by a set of questions. I would circulate to talk to the groups, but to the class as a whole I would make just the briefest introductory and concluding comments.

This experience of using the method in a three-hour block convinced me that it could be developed to teach 'efficiently' a large class for such a time. However student evaluations indicated that many found it too difficult to maintain the necessary concentration. Though I had some success in devising longer and more varied tasks I decided that the method worked best in the conventional 60 minute slot.

The final development which is of possible significance to others is my attempt to use the method when teaching two separate classes of some 600 students in an introductory 100 level class in an American state college.

Though I slightly modified my approach to try and deal with the size of the class (eg using a portable microphone), essentially the class was initially taught in a tiered lecture theatre as described above. The mid-term evaluation produced a very varied set of responses. About a third eulogised about the method, a third were not particularly positive or negative but another third poured scorn on the method. They did not see the point of it as, among other things, they did not get many facts to revise.

Though the comments were similar to those I expected at this stage of the course, the critical comments were so many and so strongly expressed I decided this was not the normal response. The approach was modified to ask more direct questions and to encourage the teaching assistants to get into the groups as they worked on tasks. However some resisted saying they felt uncomfortable approaching students they did not know.

By the second term I had essentially abandoned the method and lectured in a more conventional manner. I am still unsure what conclusions to draw from this experiment. It may be that the size of group and lecture theatre, which prevented me getting in and around many of the groups, weakened the effectiveness of the method. However, though I see myself, and others (eg teaching assistants), getting into the groups as desirable, I don't see that as essential. Rather, students have to recognise and value the point of them learning that way. Certainly there is no cultural problem in North American students adopting a method that requires them to discuss issues! Indeed, that year I very successfully used the method in teaching 150 students in a 200 level course.

I now consider that the central reason the method didn't work in the mass class was that as a visiting lecturer I (quite sensibly) only had control of the lectures in that class. Others controlled the assessment system (multiple choice questions with an emphasis on factual recall), directed the teaching assistants and what happened in labs. By contrast in the 200 level class I had control over the whole of the course and I particularly ensured that the assessment system matched the strengths of the structured lecture. So it may well be that given the right circumstances the method would work effectively with very large groups. However, it may be that such courses require very different 'solutions' to the problems posed by size.

Conclusions

I am convinced by experience that the structured lecture provides one effective design solution to the problems of large classes. The key features of the method are the division of the lecture into segments in some of which the main activity is students working on tasks decided by the teacher. It is a method which can enable students in large lecture-based courses to reach the higher level goals commonly associated with smaller discussion-based courses.

However, as has been emphasised, many students initially have difficulty in adjusting. Even at the end of the course a few students may reject it and prefer the structured information and more definite approach of the conventional lecture. For the method to succeed with the majority of students, teachers and students have to appreciate that it embodies different learning goals and a different role for the teacher than does the conventional lecture. From being a presenter of information and ideas the teacher becomes a manager and facilitator of learning tasks. To the extent that learning information is important as a course goal this is largely achieved by assigned reading outside class. Limited and valuable classroom time is used to develop student competence in higher level goals. Though in its full form as described here it does require some teachers radically to change their role, one can move to the method slowly. By introducing the occasional activity in conventional lectures one can gradually develop one's competence and confidence in the method.

Finally in certain situations it may not be so effective. It appears to work best in the conventional one-hour slot, while with classes over about 200 some students may not be sufficiently involved. In such cases more radical solutions to the problems of class size may be required – for example, to place a much greater emphasis on the package style courses described in the next two chapters.

References

Bligh, D. (1972) *What's the Use of Lectures?* Harmondsworth, Penguin.

Bloom, B. S. (1953) 'Thought processes in lectures and discussions', *Journal of General Education*, 7, 160–9.

Gibbs, G. (1982) *Twenty Terrible Reasons for Lecturing*. Birmingham, SCEDSIP.

Gibbs, G., Habeshaw, S., and Habeshaw, T. (1984) *53 Interesting Things to do in Your Lectures*. Bristol, TES.

Gibbs, G., and Jenkins, A. (1984) 'Break up Your Lectures; or Christaller Sliced Up', *Journal of Geography in Higher Education*, 8 (1), 27–39.

Howe, M. J. A. and Godfrey, J. (1978) *Student Note-taking as an Aid to Learning*. Exeter, Exeter University Teaching Service.

Jenkins, A. and Pepper, D. M. (1988) 'Enhancing Employability and Self-expression: how to teach oral and groupwork skills in higher education', *Journal of Geography in Higher Education*, 12 (1), 67–84.

Jenkins, A. and Pepper, D. M. (1989) *Enhancing Employability and Educational Experience*. Birmingham, SCEDSIP.

McKeachie, W. J. (1986) *Teaching Tips*, 8th edn, Lexington, D.C. Heath and Co.

Chapter 5

Introduction to Law: the workbook method

Nick Johnson

SUMMARY

Introduction to Law is a first-year course at Oxford Polytechnic that increased from 75 students in 1980 to 375 in 1990. In 1980 it was taught in the traditional way through lectures and seminars. To meet the problems of class size the course was radically redesigned and based around a series of student workbooks written and designed by the course team. The chapter reviews the experience of staff and students in coming to terms with the very different demands of this radical change in course delivery.

Introduction

Academic lawyers are not known for being in the forefront of educational innovation. The black letter law tradition – whereby law is conceived as a network of given facts to be mastered, remembered and applied – marries well with a narrow didactism in which lecturers pronounce their words of wisdom and undergraduates receive them (or not, as the case may be). At its worst, predigested information is fed by lecturers to students to be regurgitated, barely masticated, in examinations.

Increasing student numbers affect all subjects, though the pressure points vary. Physicists will be quickly aware of the dangers and impracticality of crowded laboratories, whereas the lawyers' equivalent, the library, is unsupervised. The lazy law lecturer can take a smug, Darwinian approach to the competition for books. Nevertheless there is usually a lowering of expectations and the students quickly learn that the voluminous reading lists are academic virility symbols rather than genuine guides.

The course

This chapter is about the transformation of a course. The course is a first year module in the Oxford Polytechnic modular degree scheme called

'Introduction to Law'. The central aim of the course carried with it the seeds of its nemesis. Besides being the foundation course for undergraduate law students, it was the prerequisite course for any study of law in any other undergraduate discipline within the degree scheme. In addition it was a popular add-on to a first-year programme for students from disciplines as diverse as biology and economics.

The rise in numbers during the 1980s was inexorable. In 1980, the course ran with 75 students. In 1990 there were 375. The primary cause of the rise was not declining resources, nor the popularity of the course but the burgeoning development of the Modular Course. As new fields of study (half degrees) were add to the scheme, Introduction to Law was either recommended to the students or available for them to take. The increase was in non-law students who in 1990 outnumbered the law students by a factor of 6:1.

The problem

When I look back at the minutes of our early meetings, at the time when we were beginning to grapple with the issues, I am struck with the narrowness of our original views. The problem as we saw it was our inability to utilise library resources with large numbers on the course. A workbook was to be produced to obviate the need to rely on the library. We rejected the textbook option for three reasons. Firstly our course was too idiosyncratic to fit any standard text, and we were not prepared to tailor the course to a textbook. Secondly we wanted students to read quite widely. Thirdly and most importantly we wanted them to use primary sources. The primary sources of law are statutes and Law Reports. Various collections of each are held in all law libraries but it was utterly impossible for these to cope with the increasing numbers on this course. We determined at an early stage to include within the workbook such primary materials – all requiring us to obtain copyright permission.

This initial premise of the workbook as a library substitute was expanded by our discussion both between ourselves and with the Educational Methods Unit (EMU) into a full-scale revision of the course. A working group of six staff were to produce ten packages which were to replace lectures as the central core of the course. We were addressing specific legal skills in an overt and decisive manner. We faced a number of organisational problems but the revised Introduction to Law did begin the following September.

The structure of the course

Superficially, there was little change. There were still lectures though they were reduced in numbers. Our intention was to retain lectures during a transitional period. As the workbook method developed so lectures would wither away. There were small group seminars and assessed coursework.

The core of the course was the ten blocks of the workbooks. Hardly revolutionary. As one student said: 'What are workbooks but fat handouts?' The changes were insidious. They dawned on us more slowly than they did on the students.

Course preparation

Anyone who has been involved in any educational initiative knows the catalogue of difficulties faced. I won't dwell on them, other than to say finding time for discussion and production is top on the list and remission from teaching, if available, should be sought. Treble your worst fears for a reliable estimate of the time it will take.

I emphasise that time is needed for discussion in order to explore each other's perceptions of the enterprise. As co-ordinator of the project and editor of the workbooks I was struck by two things: firstly the adage that academics are talkers rather than doers was given new meaning for me. We talked around the project for months before putting pen to paper. The workbooks had become an idea which we were reluctant to tarnish with our faltering efforts. Secondly despite fairly precise agreement on structure, content, format, house styles, I was taken aback by the diversity of approach taken by different authors. These hidden conceptions of the role of the workbooks ranged along a line between treating the blocks as information sources which merely replaced the library to fully interactive materials incorporating exercises, questions, etc. While a degree of hetero-geneity of style was acceptable, the acid test we adopted was whether a significant variation from the common model would confuse the reader.

The workbooks

It was agreed that every block would have a consistent structure in terms of paragraphing and there would be copious cross-referencing. Each block would contain certain diagrammatic presentations of information, graphics, self-assessment questions and additional reading. Full Law Reports were reproduced (with permission) and detailed exercises set on them. The models, conscious or unconscious, were Open University materials.

At a late stage we realised that a student would need, in addition to the substantive parts of the course, an overall guide. A block was prepared (Block A) which gave an introduction to the course, the staff, the lectures, seminars, all seminar exercises, coursework and course regulations. In later editions the previous year's examination paper was also included. Block A was a vital co-ordinating mechanism for the whole course.

Beginning the new course

The course first ran in its new format in 1983 and at that time in the institution was seen as a trail blazer. We wanted high production values (not

	Before	**After**
Course structure	2 lectures + 1 seminar a week.	1 lecture + 1 seminar + workbook.
Lectures	Central role for lectures.	Lectures the "icing on the cake". Central role for workbook.
Seminars	Little planning. Derived from lecture title. Dependent on foibles of seminar leaders. Little preparation required by students.	Highly structured. Cloned. Active preparation and participation required from students.
Library	Limited but ineffective reliance.	No reliance apart from assessed library skills exercise.
Assessment	Relatively unstructured.	Highly structured.
Demands on students	Passive role for students.	Active role for students.
Workload	Demands build up toward examination.	Course front-end loaded; high demands in early part of the course.
Course planning	Moderate level. Seminars left to deduce their task from lecture outline.	Meticulous. Careful interrelationship of all parts of the course.
Staff costs	Moderate.	High preparation time. Small reduction in staff contact hours.

Table 5.1 The structure of the course before and after the workbook method

Students

High Motivation ◄─────────────► **Low Motivation**

Mature	18 year olds
Law students	Non law students
Autonomous learners	Directed learners

Figure 5.1 Motivation of students on the course

least because it was being sold to students) and we went for state-of-the-art (now commonplace) technology for the materials. Co-ordinating the various parts of the institution needed for production and editing each contributor's block was a nightmare. Largely as a result of our experience an integrated service for the production of materials was set up by the Polytechnic's Education Methods Unit (EMU).

During the first few weeks of the course we were getting our first impressionistic feedback. Firstly, students generally appreciated being guinea pigs and there was a 'Hawthorne effect' enthusiasm which heightened students' perceptions as to the pros and cons of the course.

Secondly, there was a fair measure of confusion as to what we were requiring of students. The students on the course were extremely diverse. They ranged from highly motivated graduates who were doing a conversion course to become solicitors, to first-year students for whom law was a peripheral discipline to their main degree subject. Some foreign students who came with expectations of formal classroom teaching found the workbook approach particularly difficult.

The source of students' confusion was the strange new role and weighting assigned to each element of the course. The expectation of most students was that courses would be structured sequentially and weighted as in Figure 5.2 (top). (Those course elements in capitals represent the parts of each course given the greatest weight.)

Students look to lectures, not just for predigested information but for clues as to the weighting of the various topics and issues, indications of the lecturers' and assessors' mind-set, verbal and non-verbal clues on the examination topics. In addition many students, consciously or unconsciously, link their enjoyment of the topic to the personality of the lecturer.

We originally planned for lectures to be the icing on the cake rather than the medium for the transfer of core information. An ambitious programme of debates, case-studies, moots and videos was constructed to give students a wider view of the course material. We found the confusion felt by many students forced us to use the lectures for reinforcement. Students would be guided through more obscure (and in some cases poorly expressed) parts of the workbook and trained in how to use them.

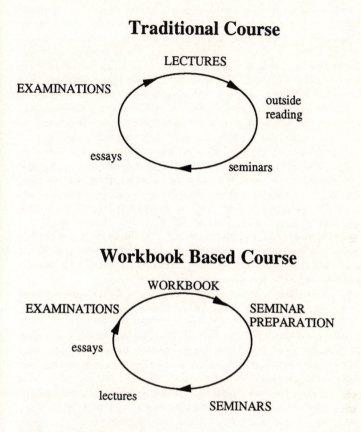

Traditional Course

LECTURES

EXAMINATIONS

outside reading

essays

seminars

Workbook Based Course

WORKBOOK

EXAMINATIONS

SEMINAR PREPARATION

essays

lectures

SEMINARS

Figure 5.2 Traditional course v workbook based course – a comparision of the emphasis placed on course components

Pushing workbooks to the centre stage of the course heightens a number of problems of interaction between the learner and the material. As one who suffered an Open University course vicariously (via my wife) I well remember the anguish of her early days on the course. The first cry of frustration was 'What on earth is the author on about?'

Not that she didn't understand the information or the factual content being transmitted: what she (and our students) wanted was the golden epistemological thread of the writer's thought processes, his or her mind-set or way of seeing the world. This desire is not an elemental academic impulse but an instrumental one. Until students know how the teacher thinks they don't know how they are being assessed.

The second cry is closely related: 'What does he or she want us to do?' The tasks which students had to perform alone were complex, some needlessly so. In our planning of the courses, besides thinking hard about methods we had considerably revised the content. We had abstracted certain elementary legal skills, mainly to do with comprehension, verbal manipulation and drafting. In our enthusiasm we had in some areas failed to sequence the students' developing skills, operated with assumptions about their knowledge and simply made the tasks too difficult. In our first revision we addressed these problems and simplified the self-assessment questions and seminar exercises. Self-assessment questions should simply test recall of the passage immediately prior to it in the text. If the questions require more effort and application than that, most readers will simply ignore them.

Thirdly, although I am no psychologist, I suspect there are differences between the ways in which the brain deals with information received through hearing and information received through reading. Certainly, there are subtle differences between speech and written form. Lecturers tend to reinforce a point by repetition, often in different ways. They can be alive to the 'atmosphere' of their audience. Cadences and dynamics in their voices can be used for emphasis and effect. The written form requires a greater degree of attention and effort from the reader although it is a better medium for the presentation of complex argument.

Finally, note taking: students' notes are a written record of their perception of the salient parts of the course. They are the students' distillations of their knowledge which, when scanned prior to the examination, should facilitate recall of those aspects of the course which are to be tested. Taking notes from workbooks needed new techniques. The workbook needed to be treated as just that, as a workbook, not as textbooks to be kept in pristine condition. In retrospect, I wish we had had put the text on alternate pages leaving the right-hand page blank for notes. A variety of highlighter pens could be used for emphasis and special attention.

Course evaluation

The course was very closely monitored by the EMU. All students filled in questionnaires on each week of the course and a representative sample of students was interviewed at similar intervals. At the end of the course, a 16 page report on the course was compiled by the head of the EMU for the course team. There were a number of interesting findings.

Polarisation

The overwhelming impression given by the replies to the questionnaires was one of polarisation of attitudes to the new course. The students were asked at each stage of the course whether they thought the aims of the course could be better achieved by traditional methods. They split pretty well exactly down the middle. From the interviews it seemed likely that those with a stronger commitment to the course (law students) were more in favour of the workbook approach whereas those with less commitment (non-law students) tended to prefer more traditional methods. There was also a marked preference for the workbook approach amongst mature students.

Time demands

The course put more time demands on students than conventional courses taken concurrently. One particularly ambitious block on law and politics was considered by the overwhelming majority to have made excessive demands. However the interviews revealed that *no* student studied for as many hours as were expected by the course planners!

Level of difficulty

Most students found the course was front-end loaded; it made greater demands on them at an early stage compared with conventional courses where the effort required early in the course was low and built up towards the examination.

Adaptation

One interesting feature both of the evaluation and of the course was the adaptation made by students over the lifetime of the course. By evaluating intensively on a fortnightly basis it was possible to observe the students on the course 'settle down'. Responses did become less polarised over the lifetime of the course, largely because the antis became less anti or reduced in number. There was a gradual warming of students to the course as their understanding of its methods and patterns increased.

Was it all worth it?

Yes. The concentration of this account has been on the teething troubles of the course most of which were addressed in subsequent revisions. In terms of effectiveness there were a number of benefits.

Staff

The staff developed a number of new skills. The planning and execution of the course heightened our common awareness of the importance of clarity and definable aims. We learned a great deal about each other's approaches to law. There was much greater cohesion and both the teamwork and workbook approach had spin-offs on to other law courses. Inevitably it was difficult to retain this cohesion over time and new staff have been noticeably less enthusiastic than the original planners. We also learned a lot about communication. Not every good teacher is a good writer and there were some tricky problems of protocol when the more obscure passages in the workbook were slashed with the editor's red pen.

Students

We were made very much aware of the different ways students learn. The autonomous learner took the course in his (or more commonly her) stride and was generally satisfied. As a vehicle for inculcating basic legal skills it was much more successful than the course it replaced. The heterogeneity of students' learning processes acted as a check on our radicalism. It seemed that the best way to proceed was to retain a multiplicity of methods. We retained seminars as an important feature and the lectures did not, as intended, wither away. The larger the group, the more important it was to retain a variety of teaching modes.

Effectiveness and efficiency of lectures

I am struck, and still surprised, by the enduring potency of the lecture. As I clip my microphone onto my tie, turn from the cinemascope sized overhead projectors to the tiered masses of students like the north face of the Eiger, I wonder whether it really is worth it. The avalanche of coughing which hits me when the flu epidemic starts, the five minutes it takes off the beginning and end of the lecture for everybody to get in and out, these and other features make communication transient and hazardous. For my audience to receive all the non-verbal cues and points of emphasis I wish to make, my performance has to have shades of Rik Mayall at a Nuremberg Rally.

If the lecture scores low on effectiveness it is high on efficiency. Yet it was this part of the course we were intending to jettison. Our changes were not led primarily by the need to reduce costs. Indeed, we actively resisted it. (After all, the fact that we were obviating the need for library support in a first-year course did not justify reduction of library funding for Law.) We fought to maintain a maximum size for seminar groups of 15. Thus the net reduction in staff costs on a group size of 300 students was minimal – 21 hours a week (20 seminar hours plus one lecture) instead of 22 hours. Rather, the principal efficiency benefit was the better management of the course. The cloning of seminars to a fixed scheme made it easier to employ part-timers and they appreciated the clarity of their tasks.

The semi-distance learning mode which we originally aimed for did allow us to experiment. We did allow a small group of committed students to take the course on a full distance learning basis. They were inmates of a local maximum security prison who received telephone tutorials.

Conclusions

The need for diversity

It is vital to provide a diversity of teaching modes to reflect the different ways in which students learn. There is no one route to Rome. If we had maintained the traditional approach we were taking in the face of rising numbers I suspect the quality of the course would have suffered and its academic standard would have been forced down. Yet we could not simply discard a lecture-based course and institute a workbook-based one on a Queen-of-Hearts dogmatism. As numbers increase the difficulty of attuning a course to the differing expectations and needs of all students is magnified. A multiplicity of methods must be preserved against a background of clear course aims.

Cost effectiveness and quality control

The workbook provided a tight structure for the management of large numbers on a single course. We, rightly, began our discussions from the premise 'how do we retain quality with greater numbers?' We ended, in my view, with a course of greater quality, but one which was not much less expensive than the one we began with. Whilst I am not saying that it is impossible to cut costs and maintain quality, I am saying that fulfilment of the two aims is rarely achieved.

Class contact v workbooks

We ended with a compromise. We preserved small group teaching and replaced some large group teaching with workbooks. It was clear to us all that the addition of the written element to the course did not lead logically to the removal of the spoken part. The elements were mutually reinforcing rather than alternative to each other.

The future

The reforms were modest and were a modest success. We refined and revised the workbooks over a number of years. New staff have been introduced to them. But just as antithesis follows thesis there has been a reaction to the workbooks: the 'innovators' have decided to return to a lecture based course! Having lost the battle I have retreated into paternalism. I am earnestly and devoutly helpful, and conceal (to the best of my abilities) my private conviction that youth must be allowed its follies . . .

Chapter 6

Guided reading in biology: a modified Keller system

Ken Howells and Sue Piggott

SUMMARY

This chapter describes the introduction of a Keller Plan course. This is a control strategy (see Chapter Three) with teacher defined course objectives, a compulsory textbook and frequent objective testing to monitor student progress through the course. Class contact time is greatly reduced and lectures are few and optional. Students are made responsible for independent study within the firm parameters set by the teaching staff.

Here these principles are adapted to an introductory physiology course previously taught in a lecture/tutorial format and which had to cope with increased student numbers and much more academically varied student backgrounds. Adopting such an approach requires significant staff time and institutional support at the design stage.

Introduction

Large classes are here to stay, and we have to find ways to deal with them effectively. It is important to find effective as well as efficient ways of teaching. Most educators in higher education would agree that the quality of the students' learning experience is increasingly at serious risk from the financial constraints imposed on us. We have to find better, cost-effective teaching methods that keep what we feel are the essential attributes of this level of learning, for our own sakes as well as those of the students. In addition, these new approaches must be able to deal with a much more heterogeneous student population than before. Widening of entry bands is going to be one of the most distinctive changes to further and higher education in the next decade.

Our case study concerns a first-year one-term physiology course on Oxford Polytechnic's Modular Degree: 8104 Fundamentals of Human Physiology. This course is a compulsory element – it must be taken and passed – for our degrees in Human Biology, Cell Biology and Food Science/Nutrition, and is recommended for other degrees in the biological sciences.

The problem

The course has intakes of about 120 students in each of the two terms it runs, and these figures will no doubt increase in the years to come. The course has persistently been given low 'excitement/interest' ratings in our first year evaluation questionnaire, and generated negative comments such as: 'I've done this before at school'; 'I suppose I need this for what comes after, but it's boring'; 'I hated it at school and it wasn't much better at the Poly'; and 'I couldn't summon up any interest in it'.

Although the course does summarise some material learned at school, and for the good reason that UK A-Level Biology syllabuses vary widely in their coverage of physiology, the students seemed unaware of the increased depth of study and synthesis and integration carried out in the course. Lectures were perceived as boring, stolid and uninspiring, with the laboratory classes and tutorials receiving better 'satisfaction' scores, although bad attendance at the latter was again seen as being due to lack of interest in the subject matter.

In these evaluations, the lecturers themselves were classed as friendly, approachable, competent and knowledgeable, so it seemed that the lectures were the main problem. Previous attempts to improve the course included variation in content and approach, changing the course leader, varying the number of staff teaching on the course, and more reliance on course handouts, none of which had any appreciable effect on student perception or performance. We therefore decided to take more drastic action and replace the lectures with something better.

Alternatives

In theory, a range of alternatives is available, such as unsupervised private study, learning contracts, self-instructional systems and small group teaching. These methods span the whole continuum of lecturer/student participation and control (Brown and Atkins, 1987), and, more relevant in this day and age, have varying cost implications. Few of us would doubt that small group teaching is academically extremely desirable, and can produce excellent results. Sadly, this is denied to the vast majority of us, but what we can do is try to pick out the advantages of these different systems and create the best possible method consistent with cost-effectiveness. We started by examining what was wrong with our present system. Why didn't our lectures fulfil their intended purpose?

In a recent study on English polytechnics, Her Majesty's Inspectorate (who assess and advise non-university higher education in England and Wales) listed the main shortcomings of 'less than satisfactory provision' as:

- over-dependence on formal lectures;
- spoon-feeding which encourages passive learning;
- work lacking clear objectives;
- insufficient meaningful feedback to students;

- teaching which encourages mere recall and reproduction.

These go straight to the heart of the main criticism of lecturing – that it is a predominantly passive process which rewards rote learning and stifles independent investigation. Unfortunately, lectures are economical for large classes, and our educational heritage has placed lectures as the preferred method of instruction in higher education, despite many studies which have placed doubts on their efficacy. In introductory courses, although the subject matter is usually relatively non-contentious, we should be fostering qualities of initiative and encouraging the students to develop good study skills.

The students

Obviously such fostering is easier said than done, particularly with the increasingly heterogeneous mix of students on such courses. To use 8104 as an example, this contains modular degree students reading for a variety of degrees. About 70 per cent of them are 'traditional entry' straight from school or sixth form college. The remainder have radically different qualifications and experiences:

- ACCESS students have little or no prior exposure to further or higher education, and have attended a special course at a College of Further Education (CFE). The essential emphasis of ACCESS courses is that they concentrate on student-centred learning (using small group teaching) to develop the students' confidence and study skills as well as providing the factual basis necessary for entry into degree courses (though the former is emphasised at the expense of the latter).
- Students from our International Foundation Programme, where overseas students take a mixture of CFE and polytechnic courses as a precursor to the modular degree.
- Mature students returning to full or part-time study.

Soon we will also have students from our Four Year Science degree, which has lower entry qualifications and a Foundation Year with a mixture of CFE and first-year polytechnic modules. Other planned developments include a Passport scheme for candidates from local schools who may lack formal qualifications but show evidence that they can undertake higher education. So our first-year classes will become increasingly heterogeneous as these intakes increase in number.

Aims

Given resource constraints, our problem was to devise a teaching methodology which tackled our initial deficiencies and would also enable us to deal successfully with this mixed intake. We decided that our prime requirements were:

- Active student participation in learning to develop core study skills, integrate traditional entry and other students, generate motivation, and improve retention.
- An organised course structure for students unfamiliar with higher education.
- Some 'whole class' sessions to generate class cohesion, improve staff–student and student–student contact, and to provide overviews.
- An opportunity for students to have increased contact with the lecturer if required.
- Easy integration into our timetable.
- Resource efficiency in terms of staff hours and library provision.

The Keller Plan

A prime candidate for satisfying these criteria is the Keller Plan learning system or Personalised System of Instruction (PSI). Originally introduced for psychology teaching in the 1960s, this involves student-paced independent learning with frequent testing during the course to assess 'mastery' of the subject matter. In its original form, the student works from detailed course objectives, study guides and set texts. Surgery sessions are available for dealing with problems and the tutors or 'proctors' are students who have successfully taken the course. Students must pass the test for each unit of the course before proceeding on to the next unit, and the pass mark is set quite high (usually greater than 75 per cent) in order to satisfy one of the prime requirements of Keller teaching, that of mastery of the subject area. By satisfying this objective, the student is self-stimulated to carry on working to the same high standard with a good expectation that he or she will similarly pass the next test. Self-pacing is provided by having the tests available early or late. Since its inception by Professor Keller at Columbia University many such courses have been run, in both arts and science subjects, although the majority of published findings deal with its application to the latter.

In general, student feedback is very favourable, and the method is at least as effective as other forms of teaching (Beard and Hartley, 1984). Claims have been made for better long-term retention of material studied using Keller learning (Hartman and Stace, 1987). In terms of resource effectiveness, earlier evaluations have claimed increased costs in terms of staff time, administration and course materials (Andresen, 1988; Black and Boud, 1977; Hartman and Stace, 1987) although others have found this method to be cost-effective (Imrie *et al*, 1980; Stoward, 1976). Part of the reason for this dichotomy is undoubtedly that there are as many variations on the basic Keller system as there are educators using Keller courses, although the basic attributes of self-pacing and frequent testing to ensure 'mastery' usually remain.

Another advantage of Keller teaching is that it has been practised in the UK for some time, so help and advice is available. We were fortunate in getting invaluable first-hand advice from an experienced Keller Plan practitioner. Dr Brian Stace of Surrey University has been using this method in first-year biochemistry teaching since the 1970s, and gave us an extremely useful and instructive seminar on the theory and practice of Keller Plan teaching. As well as allaying the fears and doubts of the more conservative staff, the practical advice given was invaluable. We cannot stress too highly the value of such personal help, preferably, as in this case, from another institution. As a result of Dr Stace's advice, we also developed the self-confidence to tinker with the original Keller doctrine so as to produce a course exactly suited to our needs.

As with all introductory courses, a set text is usually advantageous, and as part of our resource requirements involved relieving pressure on the library, selection of the text became a prime requirement. Alternatives, such as producing a tailor-made workbook or, as has happened with arts and advanced courses using this method, making a resource collection of offprints and other material, were rejected on the grounds of cost and administrative workload. Fortunately there are many good texts available in our subject area, and publishers make available inspection copies if repeat course sales are likely.

The decision to go ahead

Having obtained free copies of potential texts, we wrote a short outline of what the proposed course would entail and gave this and the texts to second-year students, asking for their opinion on both the course and the texts' suitability. Rather to our surprise, the students were unanimously in favour of the course, the brighter and more assiduous students liking the potential to work independently at their own pace, and the less able being in favour of more contact time to deal with problems.

Surprisingly, two students who were subsequently admitted to the second year by the skin of their academic teeth were also strongly in favour, being quite candid in stating that a more organised and frequently assessed course structure would have stopped their procrastinating in the first year. Not surprisingly, the mature students showed the strongest support for a less rigidly timetabled course that appealed to their greater commitment and gave regular feedback on their progress. The least enthusiastic comments came from overseas students, who liked the self-paced element and frequent testing but were apprehensive about the autonomy required by a Keller Plan course.

Given the strong level of student support, this procedure was then extended to the staff in this teaching area, who were (perhaps predictably) more cautious in their optimism than the students. This feedback also produced a clear winner in the choice of text, based on its clarity of exposition rather than depth of coverage, and the publishers generously donated complimentary copies plus the full panoply of tutor's guides, test banks, CD ROMs and the like, without which no American text feels complete.

Student and staff feedback also produced a strong lobby in favour of some lecture content, possibly as overviews to the course units. With large first-year classes, it was felt that these would generate some class cohesion and identity as well as providing a forum for post-mortems of the previous unit and general feedback on the smooth running or otherwise of the course. The mature students were very strongly in favour of this.

The timetable and course design

The syllabus of the module adapted fairly easily to a Keller Plan, producing four two-week units. Some subject matter was dropped in favour of more synoptic elements to provide better integration, but this would probably have happened anyway with an orthodox course review. The existing six hours on the timetable for each two-week unit was split into a one hour overview, four hours 'surgery' time and one hour testing.

Retests can be taken in the first surgery of the next unit but otherwise self-pacing was constrained by the schedule of overview sessions. In the original Keller Plan, the surgeries followed the testing sessions, for feedback to those who had not passed the tests, and these sessions were staffed by 'proctors' who were students who had successfully completed the course. Aside from the contractual difficulties that this would have posed, both students and staff were strongly against this move, and the surgeries were therefore timetabled using staff and postgraduates. We are not aware of any Keller courses in the UK that use students as teaching aides.

Student demand for surgeries is extremely difficult to anticipate and as resource issues were a priority, we decided on self-help groups in the surgeries, based on the students' laboratory practical classes. As the students know their practical classmates, then they would attempt to sort out any problem amongst themselves before asking the tutor for help, thus hopefully obviating the unproductive situation of a long queue waiting patiently for access to the tutor.

The large numbers of students and the frequency of testing necessitated the use of multiple-choice questions for the tests. Using a mixture of true/false, multiple choice and assertion/reason questions should in theory provide a test medium which is fair but thorough.

Having thus decided the basic outline of the course, we then produced the study guides and other course material. The course booklet contained a short introduction to the theory and practice of the Keller Plan together with aims and objectives, study guides and a practice test for each unit. Following Dr Stace's advice the study guides were kept as brief as possible, so as to avoid their turning into substitutes for lecture notes. The study guides did contain 'tie-in' sections linking the unit material with the other components of the course (practicals, essay and computer simulations), which were also modified to encourage a less prescriptive and more problem-solving approach to the material.

Preview

The students were invited to a course preview in the preceding term, and about 60 per cent of them turned up. Although there was some evidence of mild trepidation, informal feedback was favourable. Again trepidation was most strongly felt by the overseas students, who do seem to prefer more rigid, tightly defined course structures. Most of the students seemed to welcome this opportunity to work at their own pace and develop good study skills, and no students felt strongly enough to de-register off the course although there were about 25 or so for whom it was not a compulsory module. We even had one arts student (reading History of Art with Visual Studies) who elected to join the course because her friend was doing it and it seemed to be an interesting way of learning. We agreed to this and she lasted for the first third of the course, signing off only because the workload of a science course was too heavy compared with her arts modules.

Evaluation

So, how did the course go? The overview lectures were relatively popular, with about 80 per cent attendance for the first two units (compared to 60–70 per cent for first-year courses using traditional lectures). Towards the end of the course, attendance declined markedly, especially in the case of the mature students. Informal feedback revealed that they had, not surprisingly, other commitments, but once they realised the level required then the unit guides provided sufficient guidance.

None of the overviews lasted longer than half an hour, giving plenty of time for discussion. If class cohesion can be measured by the messages addressed to Dr Keller which were found on the blackboard prior to the overviews, then they served this function. The overviews were considered to be a mild success and worth retaining.

Surgery attendance was poor from the start (six to eight out of 120), and neither informal nor end-of-course evaluation revealed any perceived need for heavy surgery use. Those students who did attend needed help with conceptual problems and it proved to be the poorer candidates who attended regularly.

The practice tests proved universally popular, and some students asked for extra ones, although informal feedback suggested that they were using them as an adjunct to the course guides rather than under test conditions, so we stopped giving extra questions.

End of course evaluation revealed that the unit tests were seen as fair. The original Keller system set a high arbitrary pass rate of 75 per cent, but the course team decided to assign pass grades separately for each unit. In practice it proved quite easy (though difficult to define) to determine a mark beyond which the students were judged to have acquired the relevant level of knowledge as set out in the unit objectives. Pass rates were 80–90 per cent on the first test with most of the remainder passing the retest. Those who did not were very poor or unmotivated students who without exception also failed their first year.

Towards the end of term test attendance fell, as coursework for other modules took priority; one solution for this would be to include the tests in the assessment scheme for the module. Evaluation showed that the students were unanimously in favour of this, so we are amending the assessment accordingly. In the original Keller Plan the unit tests are the only assessment.

Student evaluation

A small group of students were chosen at random after the formal evaluation and asked for their recollections of how they spent the time allocated to the module. The general feedback was that they worked rather more regularly on the objectives than on work for other modules, devoting a set amount of time each week (usually the same as that freed by the absence of lectures), and relying on the sample test for each unit to check whether they were attaining the standard required.

An end of term evaluation questionnaire showed that the students: (a) thought that the course ran well; (b) preferred it to lectures; (c) spent slightly more time on the module compared to others they were also doing; and (d) did not perceive any noticeable improvement in their study skills. There were no noticeable differences in the answers received from traditional and non-traditional entry students.

Results

Most students showed improvements in test marks during the progress of the module, and these were approximately equal for traditional and non-traditional students. Interestingly, there were no correlations between test performance and marks obtained in the other course components (practical write-ups, essay and computer simulation analysis). Examination results showed a distinct and statistically significant increase in pass rates and average mark over the previous conventional course with more students obtaining A (70 per cent plus) and B+ (60–69 per cent) grades.

Staff evaluation

Staff feedback was also favourable, the only perceived drawback being the tight marking deadlines for the tests in order to give quick feedback to the students. The use of computer-assisted optical mark reading of test answers, using EDPAC forms, has alleviated this problem to some extent, and also means that the students' marks can be available to them as quickly as possible. We have also developed greater use of spreadsheets to process and display the data, and thus allow us to monitor student progress more closely.

Current plans are to further extend the automation of the testing using Compu-Mark software on the Polytechnic's microcomputer network. In theory a bank of, say, 200 questions are available for each unit, and the computer picks 30 of these at random for each student registering for a test. A graphics capability has recently been added so that diagrams can be added to the test, but as yet we have not been able to devise a cheat-proof way of running this system. Some staff time was certainly saved, as the surgery sessions obviated students turning up at random times with questions.

But, much more importantly, staff perceived that their time was used in a more profitable way, using the full extent of their expertise to explain concepts in the overviews and problem-solving in the surgeries. Teaching on a Keller Plan course, as one lecturer remarked, is much more rewarding and less tiring than running a lecture course. Another advantage from the lecturer's viewpoint is that feedback is available much sooner, so that remedial action can be taken.

These all add to the 'quality of life' of the teaching week, and were seen as a welcome change from tedium and a chance to use high-level skills instead of imparting factual information. The time saved can also be used simply to get to know the students better, for example just by chatting to them at the end of the overviews; a tactic much appreciated by our students and mutually rewarding to both sides. From this point of view, our experience of a Keller Plan course is that it does save on resources in that it does not misuse an institution's greatest asset: its teachers.

Developments

We have recently run another first-year module using the Keller system, this time using a workbook in place of a set text. Although the resource provision (in terms of staff development time) is significantly greater, the opportunity to design course material so as to reflect more strongly the problem-solving ethos of student-centred learning far outweighs the dis-advantages.

Indications so far are that this approach works well, as judged by greater student enthusiasm for the learning process and good progress (ie test marks). This module has also produced a low attendance at surgeries, which is our main area of concern. The more able students very quickly find out the level of work required, and quite rightly realise that they do not need the surgeries. Our evaluation revealed that students spend slightly more time on Keller modules, so perhaps the solid mass of middle-ability students work harder at this course and they also do not need to come to the surgeries. This still leaves us with many more 'problem students' than the six to eight students who did regularly turn up.

It would be good to report that the new course is fulfilling one of its main aims, and that the procrastinators are being caught relatively early in the term and mend their academic ways, joining the ranks of the workers. But, sadly, this is not so. Our experience suggests that, as with other courses, they just drop from sight and we don't see them until the end of term, when they do just enough to scrape through. With our modular course it is not possible to know with certainty the final enrolment on a particular module until after the third week of term, so with large numbers this raises additional difficulties in tracking students.

One solution to the problem would be to make the tests compulsory by either eliminating the end of term exam, (though this might penalise slow starters, and thus perhaps mitigate against mature students) or insisting on a pass grade for the Keller tests as a prerequisite for passing the course. Assessment on the original Keller Plan consists entirely of the unit tests so it is not possible to progress without taking and passing them.

Conclusions

Our experience with this type of learning has convinced us that modifications of Keller teaching can offer a real contribution to some of the problems encountered today in higher education. The initial impetus that started our work in this area was a need for a method that improved the poor performance of our students on first year modules. Science courses' wastage rates are significantly higher than those for arts and social sciences. Additionally, our widening range of entry bands is giving us an increasingly heterogeneous student population, with different commitment levels, attitudes and work patterns.

Our version of the Keller Plan has enabled us to provide a course strategy that can encourage good study skills, promote independent learning, and can be run with large classes without any loss in the quality of the learning experience and with no increase in staff teaching input. As with all modifications to teaching, it needs resources in terms of staff development time, but fortunately most institutions are much more aware than they used to be of the need to provide funding in this area.

The Keller course, which needed a workbook, did require a substantial staff development input, but it has focussed our ideas on producing a textbook in this area. Once up and running, Keller courses are no more expensive than traditional teaching methods, and freeing staff from lecturing is a valuable exercise in itself, giving them a much-needed stimulus and opportunity to re-examine their roles as teachers. Our experience with this method has given us much useful knowledge of the essentials of the teaching process, and, no less important, an impetus to change our teaching in order to face with confidence with what lies ahead.

Acknowledgement

This work was carried out as part of a TEED programme, 'Widening access to higher education, science and mathematics', managed by Focus Consultancy.

References

Andresen, L. (1988) *Lecturing to large groups: A guide to doing it less but better*. Occasional Publication 24, Professional Development Centre, University of New South Wales.

Beard, R. and Hartley, J. (1984) *Teaching and Learning in Higher Education*. London: Harper and Row.

Black, P. J. and Boud, D. J. (1977) 'Counting the costs', in: Bridge, W. and Elton, L. eds *Individual study in undergraduate science*. London: Heinemann Educational.

Brown, G. A. and Atkins, M. (1987) *Effective Teaching in Higher Education*. London: Methuen.

Hartman, G. C. and Stace, B. C. (1987) 'Keller Plan first year biochemistry', *Biochemical Society Transactions* 14, 471.

HMI (1989) *The English Polytechnics*. HMSO.

Imrie, B. W., Blithe, T. M. and Johnston, L. C. (1980) 'A review of Keller principles with reference to mathematics courses in Australia', *British Journal of Educational Technology* 11, 105–21.

Stoward, P. J. (1976) 'Self-instruction through reading; the Keller Plan', *Medical Education* 10, 315–26.

Chapter 7

Teaching Introductory Physics: techniques and resources for large classes

Ashley A. Green

SUMMARY

This chapter reports a succession of experiments to transform an introductory physics course which had increases in student numbers and the problem of enrolling students from a wider variety of disciplinary backgrounds. The increased number of laboratory sessions and reports to mark was proving an overwhelming problem for the lecturer. The case study shows how the use of student workbooks, a compulsory textbook, computer and video packages has given students a variety of options to design their own way through the course. Also, by focussing the laboratory sessions on key objectives and being more selective in what and how we assessed, marking time has been cut. A significant feature of this case study is the careful costing of the changes in staff workloads.

Introduction

The 'Introductory Physics' module in Oxford Polytechnic's modular degree course has long been regarded as an initiatory trial for new physics lecturers. Uninterested students, heavy marking and laboratory supervision workloads made it an unpopular module to teach, and the rapid turnover of lecturers as they progressed to more advanced and stimulating modules ensured that none of them had sufficient opportunity and motivation to make any major changes to it. Consequently, its content and traditional teaching methods stayed much the same throughout the 1980s.

This was the state of affairs as I found them on assuming responsibility for the module as a new member of staff in September 1988. I have delivered the module six times since then to a total of more than 300 students, which has certainly been my most challenging responsibility during my three years at Oxford Polytechnic. Class sizes more than doubled from 40 in Autumn 1989 to almost 100 in Autumn 1990.

Because some of the increases in enrolments on the courses serviced by the module (most notably the Engineering Foundation Year) have been achieved by widening access, the diversity of the students' educational backgrounds and needs has also grown. However, most of the changes to the module described in this chapter were planned *before* the recent emergence of these problems, as part of my project work for the Polytechnic's Certificate in Curriculum Development course (a one-year, part-time course for new teachers in higher education). The simultaneous intensification of these problems, with the introduction of the changes, has amply justified and hastened those changes, but the inevitable confusion of their consequences has hampered their evaluation.

I shall recount the changes in chronological order, describing their purposes, pitfalls and outcomes as I proceed, in order to manifest the iterative process by which I eventually found a satisfactory solution to the problems of large class sizes and diverse educational backgrounds and needs. For the sake of interested physicists and engineers, descriptions of the teaching resources I am using or planning to introduce are included at the end of this chapter, together with directions to sources of additional information.

Autumn 1988 term

Having just joined the Polytechnic, I ran the module my first time the same way it had been run before. I shall describe the teaching and assessment methods employed that term as background to the subsequent developments.

The entire content of the syllabus was delivered in twenty-four 50 minute lectures, over an 8 week period. A very experienced part-time lecturer gave the first fifteen lectures and I gave the remainder. These were supplemented by small-group tutorials (15 students maximum each) on alternate weeks, each student attending four tutorials on the solution of numerical problems similar to those in the final examination. Although a reading list was provided for the module, the students were neither urged to purchase a textbook nor given any specific reading assignments, with the consequence that many relied entirely on their lecture notes for revision.

The practical work for the module was performed during eight three-hour laboratory sessions. Each session's work was written up as a full report and submitted a week later to one of the supervisors for assessment. This minimised stress during the laboratory sessions, but the writing and assessment of eight reports per student (each report typically taking two or three hours to write and half an hour to mark) involved a great expenditure of time and effort, for what amounted to less than a quarter of the overall marks for the module (3 per cent per report).

Another serious drawback was that many of the students tended to rush through their experimental work without plotting graphs and performing calculations to check their results, in order to get away as quickly as possible. Consequently, poor experimental techniques, misconceptions and missing data often became evident only a week or so later, by which time such deficiencies were difficult to remedy. My immediate predecessor had made a valiant effort to foster better practices in the laboratory by issuing detailed instructions on the recording and analysis of experimental data, but most students failed to comply with these, despite having marks deducted from their reports for doing so. The most common excuses given for this were lack of time to study the instructions and a need for lectures on the subject.

Analysis of the coursework marks at the end of term indicated a rapid development of report writing skills until about the third or fourth report, after which there was little further improvement, suggesting that the later reports were rather superfluous.

I conducted a comprehensive evaluation of the module before the final examination, using a commercial software package named 'CourseView' which enabled me to set up a questionnaire with both closed and open-ended questions on one of the Polytechnic's computer systems. The students answered the questionnaire anonymously by logging into the system and keying in their responses, after which the computer generated a report containing their answers to the open-ended questions and a detailed analysis of their responses to the closed questions (in terms of their age, gender and previous experience of mathematics and physics). It was relatively easy to get most of them to complete the questionnaire during their final laboratory session and they seemed to appreciate having an opportunity to express their opinions and make some suggestions.

As expected, the students were more complimentary about my colleague's lectures than they were about mine, but many of them expressed dissatisfaction with the teaching in general. Their criticisms centred on the vastly overcrowded syllabus; the pace required to cover most of it had been too fast for the slow learners and those with little previous knowledge of physics. Their suggestions for improving the lectures included doubling the time spent on each topic (unrealistic), greatly increasing the use of practical demonstrations and relating theoretical concepts more closely to the practical work. There was a clear plea for developing their understanding of the basic concepts, at the expense of the more advanced topics. The evaluation also revealed that many of the students wanted regular unassessed feedback on how they were progressing.

Despite these criticisms, the overall marks that term were satisfactory (as they had been in previous years). Thanks to the coaching the students had received in the tutorials, most of them managed to solve the numerical problems in the examination. However, their answers to the comprehension questions revealed that many of them had attained only a superficial understanding of the topics presented in the lectures, which was hardly surprising, considering the little supplementary reading they had done. This poor grasp of basic physical concepts had been a perennial complaint from lecturers on the courses serviced by the module, and was epitomised by a remark relayed to me, by a Head of Department, from one of my students, who felt that the B+ grade he had obtained that term didn't reflect his meagre understanding of physics!

Spring 1989 term

There was insufficient time before the start of the next term for me to make any significant changes to the teaching methods, other than to produce lists of reading assignments for two strongly recommended textbooks (an excellent American introductory compendium for the physical science and engineering students and a more affordable British A-level text for the others). However, I managed to make what proved to be some very successful changes to the assessment of the practical work.

These changes were based on ideas I had picked up on the Curriculum Development course I was taking. In order to encourage the desired laboratory practices, I required that each student keep a lab diary or 'lab notes' containing the appropriate observations, data tabulations, graphs and calculations, which had to be marked and signed by one of the supervisors before leaving the laboratory. To offset the extra work this involved, I opted to halve the number of full reports to be submitted, since only the first three or four reports seemed to be effective at improving writing skills. Each student was allowed to choose which four experiments to write up.

In order to clarify the difference between lab notes and reports and what should be included in each, and also to promote consistent marking among the laboratory supervisors (a potential problem in large classes, when several lecturers and postgraduates must share the burden of supervision and marking), I issued both the students and the supervisors with lists of assessment criteria (Figure 7.1). It had been my intention to produce explicit marking schemes, but my colleagues wisely advised me to retain some degree of flexibility in the allocation of marks.

These changes encouraged more careful and methodical experimental work and recording of data, and were welcomed by students and supervisors alike. However, the resulting transformation in quality of the practical work, and halving of the number of full reports to be written and marked, were achieved at the cost of longer and more stressful laboratory sessions, with students queuing far into the lunch hour to have their lab notes marked. A pressing need for lectures and tutorials on recording and analysing experimental data manifested itself, as supervisors became inundated with questions on tabulating data, plotting graphs, estimating error limits, etc.

Nevertheless, these difficulties were generally considered to be worth enduring for the benefits attained (especially the halving of time spent marking lab reports). The assessment of the practical work has therefore

ASSESSMENT OF LAB NOTES

Lab notes for the experimental work in this module should include **graphs** and **calculations**, and must be marked and signed by one of the supervisors before leaving the laboratory. A maximum of ten marks will be awarded to each set of notes. Your lab notes should include the following:

- Complete heading, name, date and legible writing **in ink**
- Neat tabulations of data **with units** and (where applicable) informative and unambiguous comments and observations
- Estimates of error limits on all measurements
- Properly titled, scaled, labelled and plotted graphs
- Neat, intelligible and correct calculations

ASSESSMENT OF LAB REPORTS

At the end of the laboratory sessions in the fourth, sixth and eighth weeks of term, a complete **lab report** (including the original **lab notes**) must be submitted to the appropriate supervisor for assessment. This will be marked and returned to you at the beginning of the next lab session. A maximum of ten marks will be awarded to each report (in addition to those previously awarded to the lab notes). Your report should include the following:

- A concise abstract, summarising the most important results and conclusions in the report.
- A clear description of the experimental procedure.
- Simple, informative diagram(s) of the apparatus.
- A statement of results, giving values, error limits and units.
- Correct conclusions, demonstrating a clear understanding of the theoretical principles involved.
- A discussion of the theoretical principles, citing references.
- A discussion of error limits on **all** calculated values, with suggestions for improving the experimental method.
- Neat presentation with correct grammar, spelling, etc.

Figure 7.1 Assessment criteria

continued much the same since these changes were introduced. The number of full reports to be submitted by each student was further reduced to three in the Autumn 1989 term and the laboratory sessions were subsequently decreased to seven to make room for a computer courseware exercise.

Autumn 1989 term

My next priority was to implement changes in the teaching methods that would greatly reduce dependence on lectures and develop the personal study skills that are essential to the mastery of any subject. I was motivated in this by my own conviction and experience that a thorough understanding of new concepts is more effectively acquired through independent study than by attending lectures.

I wanted to reduce greatly the number of topics in the syllabus, but there was a limit to the changes that could be made without having the module revalidated (a daunting bureaucratic process). In any case, our physical science students needed to cover most of the existing syllabus in preparation for their more advanced modules. I therefore dropped only a few of the topics to make room for an introduction to the recording and analysis of experimental data.

Of the two textbooks I had recommended in the Spring term, the American introductory compendium was favoured by most students, mainly because it didn't assume any prior knowledge of physics (almost all British A-level texts assume the reader has a GCSE or O-level background in the subject). I therefore decided to adopt it as the standard textbook for the module.

I spent most of my summer vacation writing a 66-page workbook for use with the textbook. This contained weekly reading assignments, additional reading material, self-evaluation questions, numerical problems from past examination papers, useful charts, lists of physical constants and formulae, directions to supplementary study resources (videotapes, computer courseware, etc) and advice on organising self-help groups (Figure 7.2). The most time-consuming part of this task was the preparation of clear instructions and sample problems on the recording and analysis of experimental data, necessitated by the omission of these topics from the textbook.

On the Curriculum Development course, I had been introduced to the 'teach–test' technique developed by Terry Vickers at Trent Polytechnic in the UK (Vickers, 1984). This method involves the students studying on their own, using a standard textbook and a study guide or series of handouts giving weekly learning objectives, reading assignments, etc. At the end of each week the students are given a multiple choice test on that week's topics, after which the teacher states the learning objectives for the next week and gives a brief overview of the new topics to be covered. It is very similar to the Keller Plan, with the important difference that the assessment is not based

<u>Week 2</u>

MOTION

STUDY ASSIGNMENTS

Read pages 33–45 of "Patterns in Physics" and attempt some of the problems on pages 45–47 until you are sure you have understood all the concepts introduced in chapter 2. (The answers to the problems are listed near the end of the book, on pages 458–459.)

Then answer the following self-evaluation questions and check your answers against those listed at the end of this workbook.

Finally, attempt the numerical problems on pages 19–22 of this workbook, in preparation for your next tutorial.

SELF-EVALUATION QUESTIONS

Q2.1   A car travels 30 miles at an average speed of 60 mph and then travels 30 miles at an average speed of 30 mph. Its average speed for the entire 60 mile journey is:
   a. 35 mph   *b.* 40 mph   *c.* 45 mph   *d.* 50 mph   *e.* 53 mph

Q2.2   An object is released from rest and falls a distance H during the first second. How far will it fall during the next second?
   a. H   *b.* 2H   *c.* 3H   *d.* 4H   *e.* H^2

Q2.3   How long would it take a racing car to increase its speed from 10 m s^{-1} to 30 s-1 if it does so with constant acceleration over a distance of 80 m?
   a. 2.0 s   *b.* 4.0 s   *c.* 5.0 s   *d.* 8.0 s
   e. uncalculable since the acceleration is not given

Q2.4   Which of the following statements is correct for an object released from rest, assuming that the acceleration due to gravity is 9.8 m s^{-2}?
   a. the acceleration of the object is proportional to its weight
   b. the average velocity during the first second is 4.9 m s^{-1}
   c. the acceleration changes by 9.8 m s^{-1} every second
   d. the object falls 9.8 m during the first second
   e. the object falls 9.8 m each second

Q2.5   Which one of the following situations is impossible?
   a. a body having constant velocity and variable acceleration
   b. a body having constant acceleration and variable velocity
   c. a body having zero velocity and non-zero acceleration
   d. a body having velocity east and acceleration west
   e. a body having velocity east and acceleration east

Figure 7.2 Sample page from the student workbook

on the multiple choice tests but on an examination. The multiple choice tests are intended to encourage the students to keep to the study schedule, to provide them and their teacher with some indication of their progress and to reveal any specific learning difficulties and misconceptions they may have.

The teach–test technique seemed to address the very problems of dependence on lectures, lack of development of personal study skills and sporadic monitoring and provision of feedback on progress which were besetting the Introductory Physics module (indeed, the technique had been developed in the context of first-year science and engineering courses). I therefore decided to give it a try. I prepared eight 20-question multiple choice tests (similar to the self-evaluation questions in the workbook) and obtained a supply of optical mark reader (OMR) forms on which the students could record their answers for computerised assessment and analysis.

I implemented the teach–test technique as described above, with just one modification: I conducted the multiple choice test on each week's topics during the first timetabled 'lecture' period the following week, to enable the students to prepare for it over the weekend. The OMR forms were processed, graded and returned to the students at the beginning of the next lecture period, which I utilised to review the test and deal with any common misconceptions revealed by it. These regular test and feedback sessions were supplemented by weekly small-group tutorials to deal with individual difficulties and work through solutions to the numerical problems in the workbook.

I had intended to utilise the third timetabled lecture period each week as a 'surgery hour' during which I would be available in my office to give individual tuition to those who wanted it. However, by popular demand I ended up using this period to give a lecture on the key concepts in that week's reading assignments. In addition, the course tutor for the Engineering Foundation Year requested that his students be given a supplementary lecture each week, because many of them felt they needed extra tuition. This obviously defeated one of the main purposes of the teach–test technique and involved me in even more teaching than before. Perhaps I should have adhered more resolutely to my original plan, but I felt obliged to fulfil the expectations of my students and colleagues.

I realised from the outset that successful implementation of the teach–test technique would be contingent upon the provision of suitable supplementary study resources that could assist the students (particularly the slower learners) to gain a deeper and more intuitive understanding of abstract physical concepts than would be possible from written explanations alone. To this end, I had embarked the previous year on a quest for high quality video and computer courseware resources, which led to my involvement in the Open University's 'Flexible Learning Approach to Physics' (FLAP) project and the UK Computer Board's 'Computers in Teaching Initiative' (CTI) Physics Information Centre at the University of Surrey.

At the beginning of the Autumn 1989 term, I spent an entire day at the Open University's headquarters, viewing recordings of all 16 of the TV programmes in their 'Discovering Physics' (S271) course. Unfortunately, most of these programmes focus on specialised topics which are not in the syllabus of the Introductory Physics module.

A more promising source of suitable video resources was the highly acclaimed college-level introductory physics telecourse, 'The Mechanical Universe . . . and Beyond' (TMU), produced by the California Institute of Technology and the Southern California Consortium (SCC). I was the first person in the UK to express an interest in this course. During the summer, SCC notified me that a German company, Telepool, had just been appointed European distributor for TMU. Before the end of the Autumn term, Telepool's UK agent obtained two sample TMU programmes for me to evaluate. I showed these during specially arranged (and well attended) seminars shortly before the final examination. Most of the students who saw them thought they were very helpful, informative and enjoyable.

My first experience of using computer courseware was not so encouraging. Our library had maintained a fairly comprehensive collection of computer-assisted learning (CAL) packages for the BBC microcomputer since 1985, but little use had been made of it (owing largely to a general lack of awareness of its existence). At my request, the library transferred the physics courseware to one of our undergraduate teaching laboratories for use on our few remaining BBC microcomputers. I drew the attention of my students and colleagues to its availability and listed all the titles at the back of the workbook, but no-one utilised this valuable resource. This corroborated the experience of Professor John S. Risley of North Carolina State University, who has used physics courseware in his undergraduate teaching since 1983. In his *Using Physics Courseware* (Risley, 1989), he says: 'We quickly learned that students will not use a computer courseware facility or physics courseware unless their attendance is monitored and their assignments graded'. Quite so!

The new teaching methods were especially welcomed by part-time students who couldn't attend some or all of the lectures. The overall marks obtained that term were somewhat lower than in previous years but were nonetheless encouraging. Few students failed the module and several (including the part-timers) did very well. The examination paper had a higher than usual proportion of questions that tested comprehension rather than recall, which may have accounted for the lower marks.

Spring 1990 term

There was insufficient time during the Christmas holidays for me to make any further changes to the teaching methods. I therefore ran the module after the vacation exactly the same way as before. The only significant difference was in the composition of the classes. The great majority of those who take the module in the Autumn term are physical science and engineering students, but most who take it in the Spring term are from other courses in which the need for a sound grasp of basic physical concepts may not be so obvious. This is the only credible explanation which has been offered for the poor attitudes and motivation exhibited by a large minority of the students that Spring term. Many of them evidently resented being expected to purchase and study a large physics textbook, and declined to do so. The test and feedback sessions were so poorly attended that I (reluctantly) substituted lectures for them halfway through the term, but this didn't effect a noticeable improvement in attendance (presumably because many of the students had given up hope of passing the course by then).

Anticipating trouble, I conducted another comprehensive evaluation of the module, using the same 'CourseView' package as before. This revealed that many of the students wanted more lectures, particularly on the material they were meant to be learning from the textbook. The latter was strongly criticised for its size, cost and verbosity. Comments included: 'Find a textbook that explains the material instead of just going on and on' and 'The book has not left my shelf since week 1 – basically because I do not wish to be taught like the Open University!'

The overall marks obtained that term exhibited a bimodal distribution: the better students did very well (one part-timer obtained 88 per cent) while many of the weaker ones (40 per cent of the class) failed the module. It was evident that most who failed had given up trying to learn anything after the first or second week and had done little, if any, preparation for the final examination. I was obviously mistaken in my expectation that the weaker students would spend the extra time allowed by the teach–test technique to attain the required level of understanding. Most of them needed to pass the module so I had to give them the lectures they wanted early the next term, to prepare them for their resit. This was a particularly onerous task, as I already had a very heavy teaching load in the Summer term.

Autumn 1990 term

By now, I was convinced that there was no way I could satisfactorily teach all of the existing syllabus in the time available, to students who were new to the subject. During the Spring term, I had drafted a much smaller syllabus in consultation with lecturers on the courses serviced by the module. This was submitted for revalidation as part of a package of proposed changes to the other first-year physics modules that would have enabled our physical science students to cover the topics dropped from the Introductory Physics syllabus. Unfortunately, the package as a whole was rejected, though nobody objected to my new syllabus. I decided to press on with the latter regardless, for the sake of the many students who enter the module with little previous experience of physics.

I spent many hours that summer examining dozens of introductory physics compendia and A-level texts in the large bookshops in Oxford and London. I eventually found a compact and inexpensive British text (Bolton, 1986) that didn't assume much prior knowledge of physics.

With hindsight, I decided to replace the weekly test and feedback sessions with lectures (for the sake of the weaker students) but to retain the multiple choice tests as an optional feature in the workbook. This provided a choice of study modes to suit different needs and aptitudes. The change of syllabus and textbook necessitated an extensive revision of the workbook, which I completed just in time for the Autumn term.

Since the previous year, I had been working in the Open University's FLAP design team and helping Telepool's agent assess the potential UK market for 'The Mechanical Universe'. During the Easter vacation, he had obtained a set of the recently completed 'Mechanical Universe High School Adaptation' (MUHSA) videotapes which he allowed me to copy for evaluation during the next academic year. As a result of favourable evaluations by myself, other members of the FLAP design team and the Institute of Physics, Yorkshire Television decided to prepare a repackaged version of MUHSA (simply named 'The Mechanical Universe') for the UK market, which was launched in April 1991.

The MUHSA videotapes proved to be ideal for illustrating abstract concepts in lectures and supporting independent learning. I had two sets of copies made for use in the library, and included descriptions of their contents in the workbook. They are very popular with our students and are now being utilised in several of our other physics modules.

Through my involvement in the CTI Physics Information Centre, I found a useful courseware package on 'Experimental Measurements and Errors' in The Institute of Metal's 'Engineering Materials Software' series. I obtained the Institute's permission to make copies of the floppy disk and worksheets for my students. Producing enough copies for the almost 100 students who took the module in the Autumn term was a major undertaking. I substituted this courseware exercise for the first laboratory session and collected the worksheets afterwards for assessment.

The exercise involved logging into one of the Polytechnic's many IBM compatible PCs, inserting the floppy disk, negotiating some menus and working through a series of instructions, questions and problems on significant figures, sources of error, mean values, standard deviations and combining errors. The students recorded their answers on the worksheets provided. Logging in and selecting the correct menu options proved to be the most difficult parts of the exercise for the computer novices; after they had mastered these skills, the rest seemed relatively straightforward. Many of them enjoyed the exercise and found that it not only helped them grasp the basics of data analysis but also dispelled their fear of computers. It reinforced their classwork on the recording and analysis of experimental data and better prepared them for the laboratory sessions, but these benefits were achieved at the cost of several days of tedious marking of their worksheets.

The overall marks that term were significantly better than the previous Autumn's (despite relatively low attendances at the lectures and a high proportion of comprehension questions in the examination), indicating that the textbook, workbook and supplementary resources had been utilised as intended. If the examination non-attenders were excluded from the calculations then the average marks were the highest since the start of the innovations. Furthermore, whereas in the past the Engineering Foundation students had done worse than average, this time they did better than average, and very much better than in the past, and mature students excelled. Most of the students had bought the textbook and several self-help groups had been formed (particularly in the Engineering Foundation Year, for which I was now course tutor), in accordance with the advice given in the workbook.

Spring 1991 term

I ran the module after the Christmas vacation exactly the same way as before. Many of the students bought the textbook and some formed self-help groups. The overall marks that term were better yet than the previous term's (and much better than the previous Spring's), despite even lower attendances at the lectures and another fairly difficult examination.

Several factors obviously contributed to this dramatic improvement since the previous year, including the reduced syllabus, change of textbook and introduction of the MUHSA videotapes. Presented at the start of the course with a manageable syllabus and a variety of learning resources, including a workbook, affordable textbook, videotapes, courseware, weekly small-group tutorials, self-help groups and optional lectures, most of the students probably realised they had sufficient opportunity and ability to master the subject matter, and soon discovered they could do so quite effectively on their own.

Future plans

In Summer 1991, I had a new 'Basic Physics' module validated with the syllabus I created in 1990, to cater for the many students who need a true introduction to physics. I took this opportunity to obtain funding for the provision of new laboratory experiments to aid comprehension of mechanics, periodic motions and basic electrical principles, since few of the old experiments still in use in the Introductory Physics module are directly relevant to the new syllabus. I also obtained funding for the purchase of a mechanics demonstration kit, as I intend to increase greatly the use of practical demonstrations in my lectures over the next few years.

	Autumn 1988	Autumn 1990
Number of students	40	100
Number of 1-hour lecture	24	24
Number of 3-hour laboratory sessions	8 x 2 splits	7 x 4 splits
Number of 1-hour small-group tutorials	4 x 3 splits	8 x 3 splits
Assessment tasks	2 problem sheets 8 lab reports 1 examination	1 CAL exercise 7 sets of lab notes 3 lab reports 1 examination
Total teaching hours	84	132
Total teaching hours per student	2.1	1.3
Total assessment hours	216	240
Total assessment hours per student	5.4	2.4
Total hours per student	7.5	3.7

Table 7.1 Teaching and assessment workloads: before and after

The Introductory Physics module is reverting to its original syllabus, to provide a rigorous grounding in physics for those who are already familiar with the subject. It will be tailored to prepare our physical science students for their more advanced modules, though it will still be suitable for anyone requiring a challenging 'overview' of physics.

I am continuing to search for high quality physics courseware, which I shall obtain and try out as funding and time permit. I am also monitoring developments in 'interactive multimedia', with a view to experimenting with these potentially very powerful and versatile educational tools when the technology matures and suitable physics packages become available.

Looking further ahead, I shall probably substitute some of the Open University's FLAP independent study resources for the textbook and workbook when they become available (in 1994/95 subject to funding).

Conclusions

The principal changes I have made to the Introductory Physics module, in order to cope with the large class sizes and the diverse educational backgrounds and needs of the students, may be itemised as follows.

| | Autumn 1988 | Autumn 1990 | |
		Lecture Mode	Independent Study Mode
Lectures	3 hours	3 hours	
Laboratory period	3 hours	3.5 hours	3.5 hours
Small- group tutorial (average)	0.5 hour	1 hour	1 hour
Lab report	2.5 hours	1 hour	1 hour
Additional Study	1 hour	1.5 hours	4.5 hours
Total	10 hours	10 hours	10 hours

Table 7.2 Weekly student workload: before and after

1. By identifying what is and is not effective at improving experimental, analytical and report writing skills, I have been able to halve the assessment workload by replacing superfluous lab reports with the more effective use of lab notes.
2. I have greatly increased the provision of learning resources (workbook, videotapes, courseware, etc) and encouraged their use as an alternative/ supplement to the lectures, in order to promote the development of personal study skills and provide a choice of study modes to suit individual needs and aptitudes.
3. I have enabled students to obtain regular feedback on their progress through the multiple choice tests and numerical problems in the workbook, weekly small-group tutorials and on-the-spot assessment of their practical work.
4. I have encouraged students to assist one another by studying together in self-help groups.

I have managed to keep my teaching workload at an acceptable level (see Tables 7.1, 7.2) despite the rapid growth in class size, by providing small-group and individual tuition only to those who want it. I have found that I can afford the time to run weekly small-group tutorials because only about a third of the students actually attend them, so it isn't necessary to have more than two or three tutorial 'splits' each week. The other students seem to gain sufficient feedback through the multiple choice tests and numerical problems. I have tried running 'surgery hours' to provide individual tuition for those who want it, but found that only the more able students avail themselves of this resource (ie those who least need it). I find it easier to invite such students to make appointments to see me when they want to.

I have found that no single learning resource or mode of study suits everybody. Many students feel a need to have lectures available to them, but few attend lectures after they have gained confidence in the alternative modes of study. Most students find the MUHSA videotapes helpful, informative and enjoyable, but some dislike them. A minority of students will form self-help groups when encouraged to do so, but the majority prefer to study on their own. Those who do participate in such groups generally regard them as being beneficial and enjoyable. Few students will use computer courseware unless required to do so as part of their assessed coursework, but good courseware can dispel their fear of computers and be a very effective learning tool.

In summary, I have found a solution to the problems of large classes to be the provision of a variety of learning resources and modes of study involving regular feedback, supplemented by small-group and individual tuition for those who want it. This I have combined with the provision of explicit assessment criteria, and on-the-spot marking and feedback in laboratory sessions.

References

Bolton, W. (1986) *Patterns in Physics*, 2nd edn. McGraw-Hill: Maidenhead.
Risley, J. S. (1989) *Using Physics Courseware*. Department of Physics, North Carolina State University.
Vickers, T. (1984) *The Teach-Test Technique*. Birmingham, Standing Conference for Educational Development Services in Polytechnics, Joint Publication No. 1.

Resources

Video
Caltech's 'The Mechanical Universe ... and Beyond' (TMU) physics telecourse consists of 52 half-hour programmes which employ historical reenactments, close-ups of experiments and superb 3-D animated graphics (created at the Jet Propulsion Laboratory) to teach college-level introductory physics in a way that holds the interest of most students. The telecourse is supported by a set of excellent textbooks, instructor's manuals and study guides. US educational institutions can obtain a complete set of video recordings of the programmes in NTSC format from:

'The Mechanical Universe'
California Institute of Technology
Mail Code 1-70
PASADENA

California 91125
USA

Educational institutions in other countries can obtain videocassettes of the programmes in NTSC or PAL format, either individually or as a complete set, from:
Southern California Consortium
Plaza Centre
150 East Colorado Boulevard
Suite 300
PASADENA
California 91105
USA

MUHSA (the high school adaptation of TMU) is organised into 28 topical modules ranging from 'Newton's Laws' to 'Special Relativity'. Each module consists of a 15 to 20-minute video segment, a Teacher's Guide and a Student's Guide. Each Teacher's Guide provides instructional plans, essential concepts and terminology, background information, guidance for using demonstrations, and multiple choice and essay questions for assessing student achievement. The Student's Guides include an introduction to each video topic and summaries of the key points and terminology. The modules are grouped into seven 'quads' of four modules each. The quads are available in NTSC or PAL format, either individually or as a complete set, from the Southern California Consortium. They are available in the UK in PAL format only, from:
Video Sales
Yorkshire Television
The Television Centre
LEEDS
West Yorkshire LS3 1JS

Videocassettes and 16 mm films on physics are listed, by topic, in the annotated catalogue 'Physics & Astronomy: Video & Film Resources' which can be obtained from:
British Universities Film & Video Council
55 Greek Street
LONDON W1V 5LR

Many excellent TV programmes on physics, including Philip Morrison's award-winning 6-part series 'The Ring of Truth', have been produced for the US Public Broadcasting Service (PBS). Video recordings of these are available in NTSC or PAL format from:
PBS Video
1320 Braddock Place
ALEXANDRIA
Virginia 22314–1698
USA

Computer courseware

There are thousands of commercial and public domain physics courseware packages in existence. Annotated catalogues listing many of these can be obtained from:

Physics Courseware Evaluation Project
Department of Physics
North Carolina State University
RALEIGH
North Carolina 27695–8202
USA

CTI Physics Information Centre
Department of Physics
University of Surrey
GUILDFORD
Surrey GU2 5XH

Another useful resource produced by the Physics Courseware Evaluation Project is their 'Physics Courseware Laboratory', consisting of catalogues, reviews and samples of courseware (mostly for Apple II, Macintosh and MS-DOS computers) neatly packaged in a large 3-ring binder.

An excellent US initiative is the 'Physics Academic Software' project, run by the American Institute of Physics in co-operation with the American Physical Society and the American Association of Physics Teachers. They organise the review and improvement of contributed MS-DOS and Macintosh software for teaching, laboratory and research activities in physics. Their approved software may be purchased from:

Physics Academic Software
Department of Physics
North Carolina State University
RALEIGH
North Carolina 27695–8202
USA

Interactive multimedia

'Interactive multimedia' involves the integration of multiple media such as text, graphics, pictures, animation, video, music and voice into the computer environment to provide exciting new ways of exploring, analysing and communicating information. By connecting a videodisc player and/or CD-ROM drive to a microcomputer and using one of a range of 'authoring systems' to catalogue and link information, it is possible to create, integrate and cross-reference text, graphics, animation, sound, etc. As an indication of the potential of these optical storage media, a single-sided 12 inch videodisc can store approximately 54,000 full-colour images, or about half an hour of full motion video in analog form. A 12 cm CD-ROM disk can store 600 megabytes of digital data (text, images and sound), equivalent to the capacity of several hundred high-density floppy disks. These new media enable large quantities of information to be easily accessed, transported and presented in a compelling and interactive way.

'The Mechanical Universe' is available in NTSC format on a set of 26 double-sided videodiscs, together with a supplementary index disc, a database retrieval program and two interactive lessons on 'The Law of Falling Bodies' and 'The Lorentz Transformation'. These can be obtained from:

    Kellie LaValle
    Resolution
    Annenberg/CPB Collection
    PO Box 2345
    SOUTH BURLINGTON
    Virginia 05407–2345
    USA

Other sources of high-quality NTSC video discs and interactive multimedia packages on physics and related subjects include:

    Optical Data Corporation
    30 Technology Drive
    PO Box 4919
    WARREN
    New Jersey 07060–9990
    USA

    The Voyager Company
    1351 Pacific Coast Highway
    SANTA MONICA
    California 90401
    USA

At present, there are only a few interactive multimedia physics packages in PAL format, but this situation is likely to improve considerably during the next decade. Currently available packages include 'Motion' from Anglia Polytechnic, 'Energy' and 'Radiation and Radioactivity' from British Nuclear Forum, 'Water' from The Open University, and 'The Interactive Science Laboratory' from John Wiley & Sons. Information on all available interactive multimedia packages in PAL format can be obtained from:

    European Multimedia Centre
    24 Stephenson Way
    LONDON NW1 2HD

Chapter 8

Over the hills and far away: retaining field study experience despite larger classes

John R. Gold and Martin J. Haigh

SUMMARY

Fieldwork is seen as a vital element to many disciplines. This case study reports the experience of a group of geographers who, faced with declining staff–student ratios succeeded in holding on to quality by radically changing how students learn on field courses. There are elements of control in the strategies used; for example, the use of teacher-defined fieldwork trails. Most of the strategies however are independence strategies and require students to work generally in small groups that shape their own objectives, strategies of enquiry and how they use their time. This innovation involves self- and peer-assessment and as students are largely assessed as a group the assessment loading on staff is limited. Such group work requires skilled staff support and monitoring.

Introduction

The Geography Unit at Oxford Polytechnic suffered declining staff–student ratios during the 1980s. The statistics speak for themselves: in 1980, we had an annual intake of 45 students; by the end of the decade, that intake averaged 80. Over the same period, our staffing actually decreased slightly (from 7.0 to 6.8) and in 1991 we had a staff–student ratio of 1:15.

This chapter considers the implications of these changes with respect to fieldwork – an area that is widely regarded as critically important in the education of an undergraduate geographer (Gold *et al*, 1991). It shows how we have restructured our teaching to retain as much as possible of the quality of the student's learning experience. We outline two closely related case studies which show how we have tried to encourage students to become independent investigators rather than passive recipients of information and how we have tried to prevent students from getting lost in the burgeoning mass of their student colleagues. This account describes what we have done, what we think we have gained from our approach, and what we think has been lost. First, however, it is worth considering the nature and demands of fieldwork as part of undergraduate programmes.

Fieldwork

Teachers in subjects as diverse as art, business studies, engineering, history, languages and zoology argue that students need to experience their world first hand and that field study is important. In the landscape sciences, including geology and ecology, many are adamant that an education is incomplete if it excludes first hand experience of the techniques, problems, and lore of field study.

The justifications for fieldwork are broadly similar in each case. Teachers feel that slides, videos, textbook readings, laboratory practicals, and classroom and computer simulations are just not enough. Students must get out of the classroom and become involved in the messy, hands-on work of real practice. Traditionally, this involved an apprenticeship, or 'placement', style of learning, in which the student understudies a seasoned practitioner learning first-hand skills, crafts, and tricks of the trade. The novice works alongside the professional, seeking to see what the professional sees, and do what the practitioner does.

The opportunities for using such small and intimate teaching methods, however, grow increasingly rare. Larger class sizes and resource pressures force teachers away from individual contact with, and supervision of the student. In field study, apprenticeship-style teaching, like the individual college-based tutorial, has given way to the field study equivalent of the lecture. Even in the early 1960s, it was common for geographers to extol the virtues of 'using the landscape as the blackboard'. The end product of such thinking was the 'Cook's Tour'. In this model, the class is taken, usually by coach, from one site of interest to another. On arrival, the teacher proceeds to lecture from the front of the coach and the students take notes. After perhaps pausing for questions, the coach moves on to the next point of interest. Apart from the fact that students are looking out of the coach windows rather than at a blackboard or photographic slides, the activity itself is almost identical to the standard lecture.

This type of fieldwork can cater for very large numbers. For example, in the 1970s, an 'Introduction to Physical Geography' course at the University of Oklahoma enrolled more than 600 students each semester. The course included a day trip to the Wichita Mountains which, since every student attended, required a convoy of ten to twelve coaches. Each coach was guided by a graduate student who read from an itinerary learnt, more or less accurately, in a preview guided by the course leader the week before. Riding 'shotgun' with one such coach, watching the hapless graduate student mangle the scenery and script, was a depressing experience but the students evaluated the experience very favourably. For them, the field day was a memorable novelty and, of course, learners may not know enough to recognise quality or accuracy in the information they receive.

In academic terms, such activities may seem a nonsense. In this case, all the landscape provided was a prompt for the instructor: much of the time the students did not actually look out of the coach windows, preferring instead to copy down the best possible notes. Yet, it is important to remember that even poorly designed field trips can yield direct benefits. They can help enhance the self-identity and cohesion of student groups. They can help to foster good relations between students and staff, and build greater in-depth understanding through concentrating the student's thinking on one subject area for a short but intensive period of study (see Kern and Carpenter, 1986). In sum, fieldwork may be a good thing even when its academic potential is wasted; when done well, it is a form of teaching with few peers.

Unfortunately, fieldwork is also painfully expensive for all concerned. For staff it consumes much time and energy, especially when arranging and supervising trips that require extended periods of residence away from college. Colleagues from subjects which require little fieldwork often suggest that staff time and resources might be spent in 'more cost-effective ways'. Students equally find fieldwork expensive. Increasingly forced to meet at least part of the cost themselves, they also find that their opportunities for finding vacation employment are constrained by the necessity of attending a field course.

Our response to these pressures has been threefold. First we decided that fieldwork was an essential quality element of our degree programme. It was deemed essential to our view of the education of a geographer. For students it could, if well taught, be a peak experience which would significantly affect their attitude to the more formal classroom-based courses. Politically, within the institution, we lobbied for spending on fieldwork to be maintained. When we substantially revised our degree programme we ensured that fieldwork was tightly integrated into it and thus much harder for administrators to axe. We showed our commitment to fieldwork by continuing to invest much time to preparing and working with students in the field. By contrast other aspects of our teaching were more significantly cut; for example many courses replaced some classroom teaching by learning packages. Also, while in 1980 staff were often in their offices for informal consultations with students, by 1991 students could only see staff readily during restricted office hours – unlike fieldwork such informal consultations were deemed an aspect of quality that could be cut.

Our second strategy was pragmatically to pare back our fieldwork programme (see Table 8.1). In 1980-1, Oxford Polytechnic geography students undertook 19 days' compulsory fieldwork during their three years of study. By 1991-2, this had been cut to 11 days. At the same time, we looked for ways to retain, or even improve, the pedagogic effectiveness of this reduced commitment of days spent in the field. Our approach to doing so lies in finding ways of recapturing the spirit of the apprenticeship model and applying it to the progressively larger classes and shorter fieldwork periods with which we are faced. It has been guided by a philosophy of education that holds that students learn best when they are active participants in their own education and when they are directly involved in problem solving, maturing by building confidence in their abilities to meet problems and execute solutions.

To illustrate these arguments, we present two case studies which describe, respectively, an introductory field weekend for new students and an advanced course (module) which includes training in field research methods and provision of practical experience of environmental issues. In both cases, we have adjusted to the new circumstances by promoting problem solving through group-based project work, by expecting students to take responsibility for their own learning, and by restricting the teacher's role to that of co-ordinator for the class, facilitator for each project group, and provider of technical training and guidance in the formalities of method.

A weekend in the country

The first weeks of a student's college career are a disorienting time. The introductory weekend field trip of the Oxford Polytechnic Geography programme seeks to introduce the students to one another and to the teaching staff. It also tries to enthuse them with the special aims and teaching methods of the Geography programme and to provide them with some new notions that they will need in their further studies.

The course takes place during the second weekend of the students' college careers. It spirits them away to an isolated field study centre in the Welsh borderlands and immerses them in a landscape that most find totally unfamiliar. Originally, all students and all staff joined this weekend course. Now, because of the limitations of our field centre accommodation, staff and students are divided between two parties. Inevitably, this weakens a course that aims to establish the identity of a group who will study together for the next three years. Yet, it still provides a means of giving students some points of reference in this early phase of their undergraduate studies.

From the beginning, we have used this weekend as a vehicle to introduce students to problems involving society–environment relationships – the main focus of the Geography programme. In it, we stress issues related to the ways in which society perceives landscape, assigns value to landscape attributes, and proceeds to create policies and select strategies for the management of the environment. To this, we have now added a conscious attempt to introduce students to the notion and implications of group work, one of our principal strategies to deal with larger student numbers.

	1982	1991
No. of staff	4	3
No. of students	45	78
Status	Compulsory, 3rd year	Compulsory, 2nd year
Working days	9	5
Location	Abroad (Amsterdam)	Home (Brighton)
Departmental Contribution	Complete	45 percent (1991) funding
Student Contribution	Spending money	Contribution to maintenance and meals other than breakfast
Work done prior to field-course	Minimal	Extensive
Work done after	Minimal	Formal verbal field-course and written reports
Assessment	Equivalent to 20 percent of module	One module

Table 8.1 Comparisons of Oxford Polytechnic's main geography field-course, 1982 and 1991

The point is rammed home immediately. The programme commences with an 'ice-breaker', a simulation game called Bafa Bafa,[1] which simulates the problems that arise in the meeting of different cultures with dissimilar value systems. The students are divided into two groups and immersed in two different milieux: one a frenetic, competitive and meritocratic society; the other a relaxed, non-competitive, society where status is defined by birth and gender. As the game progresses, students are sent as ambassadors to the other culture and report back on their experiences. In the final debriefing, the groups are reunited to consider how and why their respective 'cultures' accumulated information and disinformation about each other.

This simulation provides a springboard for the following day's work. Students are shown videotapes which analyse the varying ways in which the press in different countries report the same event. They are informed that they will be part of a team of 'journalists' visiting the South Wales mining town of Blaenavon to produce a story for their 'newspaper'.

The students are divided into small groups and given a sealed envelope which describes their newspaper's editorial line (a secret for their group to keep). The remits are not distributed randomly – unbeknown to the students, they have been sorted into two 'cultures'. One set is encouraged to seek stories with an optimistic character; the other seek stories with a pessimistic disposition.

This task is made easier by the fact that their visit to Blaenavon is guided by written trails to assist them in getting a flavour of the town and its post-industrial landscape, which carries the marks of two centuries of coal mining and steel working (Haigh *et al*, 1991). Student groups are dropped with their trail at intervals in the landscape. The trail provides key information on the area but it mainly directs students along a route and gets the groups to answer questions relating to what they see in the landscape.

Unknown to the students, there is not one trail, but two – these look the same and follow the same route, but contain different interpretations. Groups which are required to find positive news about Blaenavon receive trails which consistently present a sunny, forward looking viewpoint; the others receive trails that are a melancholy reprise of the past. For example, in one trail, a coal shale slope that is 50 per cent vegetated is described as showing how the damaged land has resisted colonisation by plant life for 100 years. In the other trail the same landscape is described as showing how nature is gradually repairing the scars of the past.

In the evening, the students paste up the cover pages of their 'newspapers' in separate 'newsrooms'. There, they work up an article that broadly represents their collective viewpoint. Finally, the two groups present their findings to one another. The debriefing session which follows links the exercise to the previous night's experience of Bafa Bafa. Specific comment is made about the themes of values and cultural perception, about the merits

---

[1] This simulation is commercially available in a slightly different form, 'Rafa Rafa', from Christian Aid, 240–250 Ferndale Road, Brixton, London, SW9 8DH.

of simulations as a learning tool, about the hidden agenda which guides most written communication and how to recognise such influences. Above all, the students are asked to reflect on working in a group, with an initial analysis of their day's experiences.

On the final morning, the students are beaten with another blunt instrument: a game simulation based on 'The Prisoner's Dilemma' (also known as 'Zero-Sum' or 'Win as much as you can'; see Pfeiffer and Jones, 1974, 62–87). This is intended to introduce an appreciation of the demands of teamwork. The Prisoner's Dilemma is a group based game which requires no more equipment than a blackboard and simple tally sheets. It takes about two hours to play. The game involves several rounds and one task. The students are told that 'they must win as much as they can'. Most interpret this as an injunction to win as much as they can individually, but the game is so structured that they only win by working as a collective. (Note that throughout the weekend students are allocated to different groups, so ensuring they meet a large number of their colleagues and have experience of working in different groups.) The debriefing focusses on the processes by which people work in groups and on the 'rules' which are needed to encourage trust and confidence in one another.

So this is what happens, but how do we see it as a response to our problems of increased numbers?

First it still happens. During this period (1980–91) as we agonised over which aspects of the fieldwork programme/overall course had to be cut, this introductory weekend was singled out as something that had to be retained. We decided it provided a central role in forging student identity as a group of geographers. As they return to campus they are not anonymous disoriented individuals; indeed for many this is the beginning of strong friendships and a sense of being a member of the Geography department. Student evaluations even three years later see the importance of this social bonding.

For staff the weekend is also central to acculturating students to ways of learning that will enable them to survive with limited staff support. Most students enter with the assumption that staff will tell them what they need to know. Though the weekend is carefully structured by staff, students learn by reflecting on their experience of a simulation, a fieldwork trail, etc. Students learn to work interdependently as a member of a large group, and in particular as a member of a small group, with only limited staff involvement. As we shall show in our next description, group-based projects both in fieldwork and in classroom-based courses are central ways in which we have sought to cope with more students.

Finally, the fieldwork trail provides a way in which large groups of students can learn actively in the field, drawing on the expertise of the staff who devised the trail but with limited or no immediate staff supervision. This approach provides better quality learning than the traditional 'Cook's Tour' (Keene, 1982).

A week by the sea

The other case study deals with a field course that occurs in a student's second year of study. Larger in scale but building on principles established in the first year, this field course is associated with a module called 'Geography and the Contemporary World' (GCW). GCW itself has five aims:

1. To build experience of the practical and ethical problems surrounding investigations into the interactions between environment and society.
2. To develop teamwork as a forum for active student learning.
3. To establish an ethos of inquiry that makes students less content with passively received wisdom and more capable of finding wisdom through their own endeavour.
4. To provide practical training in field research relevant to the central focus of the curriculum, most notably to help students approach their dissertations, individual investigations which are taken as the mark of honours quality.
5. To build skills which will enhance the student's future employability – including problem-solving, collaborative skills, communication and presentation skills and project management.

GCW is a compulsory module and involves our entire second-year group of around 80 students. It spans the Easter and Summer terms, with its integral residential field course occurring halfway through the module during the Easter vacation (see Table 8.2).

Before describing the field course we signal the main ways in which we have tried to cope with an increased cohort from about 40 to about 80 students. First, much time is spent preparing students for the field experience. Though the time in the field is limited our aim has been to get the maximum value from it by careful preparation and follow up work. By contrast in the early 1980s our main field course lasted longer in the field but had little preparatory or follow up work (see Table 8.1). Secondly, supervising circa 80 students doing project work is made considerably easier by requiring students to work in groups of four to six (so only 15–20 projects need be supervised), and getting students to give feedback to each other rather than the tutors carrying all the burden of the supervision. Thirdly, from a student perspective most of the time in the field, and for much of the preparatory and follow up work on campus, student groups work relatively independently of each other and the tutors. For them a dominant experience of the course is being a member of a small group.

The field course is preceded by a term spent in preparation, in which the staff help the students to focus down on a feasible research study. An early session formally guides students through the processes of group formation and teamwork using ideas from *Making Groups Work* (Gibbs, 1987). Subsequent preparatory sessions concern special topics that evaluations show produce problems: devising a project that is feasible in the time

Week	
1	Introduction
2	
3	Preparatory sessions
4	
5	Project approval session
6	
7	Tutorials (informal)
8	
9	Poster session and fieldwork briefing
10	
Vacation	6 Day Field Camp in Sussex
1	
2	Tutorials (informal)
3	
4	Conference weekend
5	
6	
7	Submission of written report
8	
9	
10	

Table 8.2 Structure of GCW field based course

available; the uses and misuses of interviews; and making presentations. Between sessions, student teams refine their topics in consultation with a staff guide. Lists of potential topics are supplied and students are advised to consider models provided by examples of the better projects from previous years. These then lead to a project proposal session, in which students justify their project not to staff but to another student group, who in turn explain it to the staff. This system requires clarity on the part of the proposing group to get their message across and has been found to increase student awareness of the work being undertaken by others. In addition, students are active in the constructive appraisal and revision of other students' project plans.

The field course follows in the Easter vacation. From 1985–91, this was at Brighton on the Sussex Coast: a location which offers a wide range of contrasting contemporary environmental issues as well as ample accommodation. The field course provides five working days and builds on the strengths of its group-based structure. Instead of days spent on staff-led coach tours or leading crocodiles of reluctant students on guided walks, the student teams work independently on their projects during the day. They organise their own transport, arrange interviews or field visits, and schedule their work so that it can be completed during the time available. There is no staff supervision of project groups in the field, unless requested to act as consultants for some specific reason or unless a group is floundering. Groups are charged with the responsibility for completing their work autonomously. To date, they have risen to that challenge.

During the day staff are largely free. They have been known to write research papers, visit stately homes, eat convivial meals as well as evaluate new project work areas – for them there can be some quality to the experience.

The class only meets as a full group in the evenings, when there are seminars and short progress report sessions. Here, too, the staff's role is limited. We arrange the format of the evening sessions and are available for consultation for any group that is experiencing problems or requiring a change in the direction or emphasis of their project. Provided that the preparatory work has gone well, only a small minority of groups need much assistance. In turn, this eases the pressure on staff, who despite having parties of 70–80 students, can devote their time to those who most need assistance and give others the opportunity to work autonomously guided by the comments of their peers.

The ensuing term is devoted to data analysis, preparation and presentation of final reports, and reorienting the class to the wider context and implications of their project work. Each team tackles two assessed tasks. First is a verbal presentation in the 'Conference Weekend' (Table 8.2) held at a centre near Oxford, when they have to represent their project to the class. Guidance is given as to what makes an 'effective' presentation. The teams respond to an element of competition in this session. Teams vie to create the best impression seeking to get their message across more effectively than their colleagues. Presentations vary widely. Some involve a straightforward talk with slides, others use simulations of various types, and yet others use plays, videos, even music. In addition, each team must act as discussants for another team. This means that they take responsibility for providing a brief verbal summary of another's presentation, highlighting points of strength, weakness or importance, and accepting responsibility for leading the discussion. Each session, although chaired by a member of staff, has a discussion period led by student discussants and continued by student members of the audience; the staff play no role in leading or stimulating discussion.

The second task is the submission of a written report from each group. This is presented as a single, scholarly research paper after the style of a dissertation. This report must include a justification for the study, a review of related writings, description and analysis of technique and method, critical evaluation of findings and suggestions for further research by future project teams.

Discussion

We began this chapter by noting our steadily increasing student enrolments. The first-year field weekend once saw six staff going away with about 40 students: now the same number of staff deal with around 80. Until 1986, that trip was free to students: they now pay over 75 per cent of the costs. Comparing our current GCW field course with its antecedent from 1982 (Table 8.1) also shows the extent to which staff–student ratios have been eroded and financial burdens shifted on to the students. In addition, the forced substitution of a domestic for an overseas location and the drastic reduction in the number of days available for the field study clearly demonstrates how fieldwork resources have been squeezed.

Our case studies both attempt to extract more from less. In some respects, we have succeeded in making a virtue out of a necessity. Designing the weekend field course around group projects has given the trip greater cohesion and serves to introduce first-year undergraduates to group work. The social dimensions seem undiminished, with classes in the weeks following the trip seeming warmer and less formal than before.

Similar conclusions can be made with regard to the larger GCW field course. Fieldwork which involves students as small project teams rather than individuals helps teachers preserve the quality of the learning experience despite increases in student numbers. It has remained possible to continue holding informal group tutorials without massive extra commitments of staff time and resources: indeed, the techniques described require less formal staff input and allow greater personal contact with students – albeit as teams. The approach demands relatively small amounts of working space, except in the field, so it adds less stress to overstretched college resources. It is welcomed by students who appreciate the informality and freedom that the system provides – even at the expense of the stresses incurred in learning teamwork skills. It encourages students to become better investigators, more active in their learning, better at verbal presentation and, if our contacts with the world of business are accurate, more employable. Finally, there are benefits to all concerned in terms of assessment. Students are able to participate in the assessment process and gain critical insight into what is valued, whereas the staff gain from the greatly reduced loading of assessing students as teams rather than individuals.

That much is certainly positive, but it would be wrong to give the impression that adopting these techniques solves all the problems of large classes. They do nothing to relieve the logistic problems of accommodating and resourcing a field camp. Furthermore, because of the open character of project selection, the approach places increased stress on technical and equipment resources.

In addition, the group work and project-based approach carries its own problems. It can encourage student teams to focus too closely on their individual project and to neglect wider issues. Providing an overall class focus, supported perhaps by forcing interaction between teams, as in our discussant system, or by saving part of the assessment for an overall evaluation of general linking themes is necessary to redeem this problem. Perhaps most important, there are dangers in overusing group approaches as a response to large student numbers. It does not suit the tastes and needs of all individuals and is prone to abuse by student freeloaders. Students also become bored by being constantly faced by the same demands. Any course that employs group work needs to consider carefully how much group work also figures in other parts of the students' programmes and how its use in different courses can be dovetailed together.

Many of these problems can be overcome by careful curriculum planning. It would not, however, be fair to conclude without sounding a further warning note. Despite sharp reductions in fieldwork programmes, the demands on staff in terms of fieldwork teaching and administration remain heavy. During the academic year 1990-1, for example, half the geography staff at Oxford Polytechnic spent virtually the entire Easter vacation in running duplicate field courses. Teachers who also run optional field trips as part of their modules can lose as many as five or six weekends in a term due to large class sizes. That type of pressure cannot be sustained permanently. We are conscious, too, of the mounting financial burden on our students. The day is approaching when they may have to meet the entire costs of fieldwork. This may affect recruitment, with poorer students voting with their feet in favour of subjects that do not impose this additional financial burden. In turn, this could further diminish the amount of resources coming to subjects with large field course commitments.

We have already stripped our own fieldwork programme down to the bare minimum. Informal contacts indicate that colleagues elsewhere, in geography and in other disciplines, have adopted similar strategies. Large class sizes and straitened times may well have acted as stimuli towards finding more productive and cost-effective methods of fieldwork teaching, but there remain limits to what even creativity can achieve.

References

Gibbs, G. (1987) *Making Groups Work*. Educational Methods Unit, Oxford Polytechnic.

Gold, J. R., Jenkins, A., Lee, R., Monk, J. J., Riley, J., Shepherd, I. D. H. and Unwin, D. J. (1991) *Teaching Geography in Higher Education: a Manual of Good Practice*. Institute of British Geographers Special Publication 24, Oxford, Basil Blackwell.

Haigh, M. J., Keene, P., Kilmartin, M. P. and Gold, J. R. (1991) *Blaenavon/
Blaenavon: A Welsh Valley Landscape Trail*. Oxford, Thematic Trails.

Keene, P (1982) 'The Examination of exposures of Pleistocene sediments in the field:
a self-paced exercise'. *Journal of Geography in Higher Education*, 6 (2), 109–21.

Kern, E. L. and Carpenter, J. R. (1986) 'Effects of field activities on student
learning', *Journal of Geological Education*, 34, 180–2.

Pfeiffer, J. W. and Jones J. E. (1974) *A Handbook for Structured Relations
Training*. Vol 2 (revised). La Jolla, University Associates.

Chapter 9

Study networks: support mechanisms for large groups of part-time students

Julie Hartley and Harinder Bahra

SUMMARY

The move to a mass higher education system means not just more students but also very different types of students, including many more part-time students who have to balance work and study commitments. Part-time students can feel very isolated from each other and have little chance in their limited time in college to discuss the course informally. This case study is of a part-time business studies course where staff helped students to create self-help groups which support each other through the course. This independent strategy is one that could also be adapted to courses for full-time students. Such self-help groups can take much of the tutorial and counselling load off staff. However, staff need to give guidance and support to students so they can run their groups effectively.

Introduction

This case study examines the experience of the BA Business Studies (BABS) part-time at Birmingham Polytechnic. It covers a period of change for both students and staff associated with the degree. The innovation was introduced to complement a newly redesigned degree scheme. It involved the formal introduction of student study networks, where the aim was to produce a more positive learning climate and a mechanism for mutual support and guidance. The networks form the basis of interactive work during programmed lecture time and groups are encouraged to meet outside class time, for example during residential activities and group assignments.

The innovation was introduced because of the daunting prospect of 90 new part-time students starting in October 1990. The introduction of a revised degree structure, new material and new regulations presented an interesting challenge for the course team. There were a number of dilemmas involved in the design and delivery of the new course. We needed to satisfy what appeared to be irreconcilable objectives. Firstly, there was the increase in student numbers – the new intake represented a 30 per cent increase on our previous enrolment targets. Exacerbating this situation was the fact that there was no discernible increase in resources. Secondly, we clearly wanted to maintain the quality of the programme, especially considering that there was strong competition from similar degree programmes in the West Midlands. The final pressure came from the internal restructuring of the Business School undergraduate courses. Any innovation that we introduced had to complement the standardised, modular 'Integrated Degree Programme' that was being developed across the whole Business School.

Prior to this turmoil, the BABS had been operating in splendid isolation for approximately 13 years, with no substantial change to its basic structure, objectives or philosophy. The degree has always been fairly conventional in its delivery and the usual pattern of study involves attendance at college two evenings a week for five years. The majority of units are lecture based and an average student would attend three and and a half hours of lectures per week. The timetable has always been fairly rigid; it did not encourage any interaction between staff or students and their peers.

We found that there was virtually no time available to develop college based activities. Lectures tended to be about transmitting information, so in-depth discussion and small group work were very difficult to programme. Despite these problems, the majority of students are well motivated, mature and have valuable business experience. They just need the opportunity to make the most of their strengths. In trying to capitalise on our students' obvious potential contribution to the course, we had to take into account the very real problems and constraints facing part-time students.

Problems facing part-time students

The BABS degree is typical of many part-time courses throughout the UK. Students are under enormous pressures: personal, work and academic. A recent survey conducted by some final-year students as part of an Organisation Behaviour project investigated some of the problems experienced by their peers. Two key features emerged:

- A sense of isolation and difficulties in developing support networks.
- Time management difficulties and the problems of handling multiple priorities and commitments.

This limited survey conducted in February 1991 served to reinforce formal and informal feedback received from students over a number of years.

Isolation

A major problem identified by our small survey was the sense of isolation and the difficulty in developing support networks. The course at Birmingham Polytechnic has a very heterogeneous group of students, drawn from a wide range of organisations. There is a wide geographical distribution and the spectrum of work experience is extensive.

The structure of the timetable and the predominantly lecture-based teaching strategy do not lend themselves to the development of social interaction. The timetable is very restricted, ie two evenings a week from 5.45 pm to 9.15 pm. We normally try to fit in two, one and a half-hour time slots with a half-hour break. The half-hour break is very often eroded as students negotiate with individual lecturers to start their second session 15 minutes early so they can leave at 9.00 pm. The tight schedule leaves the students very little time for informal discussion with their peers or members of staff and the social aspects of the course are extremely restricted. The irony of this is that those students who do manage to develop their own informal student self-help groups find it invaluable. We have had some first-class-honours students who attribute their success directly to an active and supportive student network. The majority of individuals, however, plough on alone. They have neither the time nor the space to build a supportive mechanism. These students lead an isolated existence and are entirely dependent on their own resources in completing the degree.

We wanted to give the students an opportunity to develop despite these problems and we realised that we needed to provide mechanisms to support their learning activity. There have been a number of developments within the units as lecturers try to integrate work experience and provide practical applications within the academic framework. However the institutional pressure for standardisation and harmonisation has meant that the problems had to be tackled outside the structure of the existing modules.

Time management

To illustrate the issues associated with time management we asked a part-time BABS student to describe a typical week. Some interesting illustrative material emerged.

1. She spent 40 hours at work, usually 8.30 am to 5.00 pm. This involved a reasonably high level of responsibility, supervising 10 people in a recently privatised organisation. She was currently having to handle lots of change in the workplace.
2. She spent two nights a week at college: 5.45 pm–9.15 pm. She attended four and a half hours of lectures per week, with one and a half hours spent in the library. She usually arrived home at 10.00 pm on college evenings.
3. She spent two nights a week and a half-day at the weekend trying to prepare for assignments. She had no time to complete recommended background reading. She felt guilty about her spouse and children who were usually on the rampage at a particularly critical or difficult part of an essay.

4. The rest of the week was spent catching up with domestic and social commitments.

This profile is by no means exceptional. Our experience would suggest that this pattern is repeated many times over with mature part-time students. These students have to try to balance their priorities and that balance is very precarious. Their multiple commitments mean that the balance is frequently upset. Illness, promotion, redundancy and family circumstances are all a major source of stress, and it is very often their academic commitments that have to give way.

It takes a highly motivated individual to pursue this kind of regime for five years. Time management and access to resources is a major issue for the design of any part-time course: it has to be flexible enough to cater for the complex and demanding lives that these students lead.

Student study networks

There was an obvious need to support and develop our students in order to overcome the problems that have emerged and to utilise fully their reservoir of experience. A major step in tackling the problem of student isolation was the development of student centred study networks. These were not a new phenomenon on the BABS part-time but their existence tended to be patchy and ad hoc.

The study networks are formally incorporated into the fabric of the degree programme in a number of ways. First of all the study networks have a clearly defined aim: Successful study networks will encourage students to support each other and encourage students to take deep approaches to learning. The study networks are seen to have two key elements:

- Study networks should provide a positive emotional and motivational learning climate and therefore enhance learning opportunities.
- Part-time degree students rarely get the opportunity to support each other on an informal basis. Study networks should provide opportunities to do this in autonomous student groups.

A number of stages were designed to introduce and maintain networks on the degree programme.

1. In the first stage students were allocated to groups using geographical criteria. As far as possible groups of students living in reasonably close proximity were formed.
2. During the Introductory Programme the groups participated in team-building exercises. For example they were asked to brainstorm the different ways in which a study network could be used. They were asked to examine the ways in which they could make a study network successful. At the end of the evening they were encouraged to share information, ie names, addresses, work/home telephone numbers. The

information was immediately photocopied by staff and distributed to all members of the group.

3. Business simulation games were run to help promote cohesiveness within groups. To improve the impact and success of these activities this was carried out on a two-day residential weekend at the start of the academic year.

4. The next stage of the programme focussed on the importance of groups and an analysis of group processes. This not only enabled students to value the possible advantages of harnessing and enhancing individual learning through doing group tasks but also required students to analyse the group's dynamics and learn about process issues. Groups that are competent in managing their own processes and agendas will ultimately be more successful in maximising the learning opportunities open to them. They will also be capable of identifying the strengths, weaknesses and contributions of each individual within the group.

A typical network building exercise might focus on:

- An exchange of relevant information, eg addresses, telephone numbers, work experiences, study experiences etc.
- A sharing of experiences and feelings about how they have managed to cope with studying in the past, ie strategies for survival.
- A simulation exercise in which participants working in their groups learn to exchange information.
- The creation of group action plans identifying specific ways in which participants are going to help each other when they are given their first assignment.

A survey of the study network was conducted in July and August 1991 to ascertain whether or not we should continue to promote study networks as an integral part of the course. The results were overwhelming. Ninety-two per cent of the students questioned were still members of a study network after one academic year. Ninety-four per cent of students thought that study networks should be encouraged on the course, and only 5 percent thought that study networks were not a useful aspect of their studies.

Most students appear to participate in a single study network. The size of the groups varies from two to eight participants – the norm is around five people. These findings support previous research into optimum size and performance of groups. Seventy-five percent of students surveyed said that their network had changed from the original group at the beginning of the course. This was to some extent inevitable as we found out afterwards that our original geographical division had broken up already established groups from work or previous studies. It was very encouraging to find out that a high number of students (79 per cent) have personal contact outside the boundaries of the Business School. By far the most frequent form of contact was by telephone (89 per cent).

It was not surprising that a core part of the study network was centred around activities of sharing information. The study network appears to act in an information brokerage role, supplying lecture notes, general materials and course information. However there were also a significant number of students (76 per cent) who saw the network as a form of mutual support and source of motivation. This idea was supported with qualitative data provided by students interviewed about study networks. They saw networks as a means of increasing motivation on the course, it was a support mechanism to keep them going and helped to prevent isolation and idleness. One interviewee remembered that it gave the members an opportunity to discuss their problems with other people and discover that they are not the only one to experience doubts.

Respondents were encouraged to evaluate study networks and to share advantages and potential disadvantages.

Advantages

- If you have a problem you can talk to other people about it.
- Different perspectives will aid your learning.
- Revising and going through helps your own understanding.
- You are not on your own.
- Sharing of information, textbooks, notes and information.
- Moral support and confidence building.
- Motivating factor.
- To help you see if you are on the right track.
- Useful when you cannot find lecturers.
- Taught you to trust and share.
- Generates ideas.
- Makes the course more interesting.

Disadvantages

- Travel and transport problems.
- Distance.
- Time to meet up, ie work pressures.
- Agreeing a location.
- Membership of networks may change.
- Members may not share work (they may want a better mark).
- If a group breaks up completely where would you get new members from?
- Sometimes not mutually beneficial as some members may not have have done their work but want to share yours.
- Groups may be too large.
- Strong dominant members may limit other members' contribution.
- May exclude members with family commitments, eg single mothers.

These advantages and disadvantages indicate a whole range of benefits and potential handicaps for students.

Activity	Resources
1. **Initial discussion** agreeing format and defining objectives	3 staff over approx 2 hours 6 hours total
2. **Planning** designing activities ie brainstorming exercises	2 staff over approx 2 hours 4 hours total
3. **Implementation**	
3.1 Sorting students into geographical areas	3 hours
3.2 Running Introductory programme	3 staff over 2 hours = 6 hours
3.3 Briefing other staff members	1 hour
Total	**20 hours**

Table 9.1 Study networks, key costs

Conclusion

It is evident that student networks are a crucial part of the learning process for BABS part-time degree students at Birmingham Polytechnic Business School. It would appear that this innovation helps students' motivation and commitment to their learning and the course. There also appears to be evidence that the process enriches and develops student academic performance with their roles as professionals in organisations.

The costs involved

This was a new development for the course so any consideration of costs must include an analysis of the development time involved in the project. Our experience is that this kind of student centred approach must be carefully planned and clearly defined. This obviously involves staff resources. The key costs can be defined as in Table 9.1.

Other activities such as running the residential weekend and setting up group assignments were part of our mainstream programme and did not entail extra resources. The main benefit of this kind of innovation is that it can be easily integrated with an existing course and implemented at very little cost, especially if you identify activities on your existing course that can be used to reinforce the networks.

What have we learned?

We are now on our second cohort of students since the introduction of the new degree scheme in September 1991. We have had a chance to evaluate this innovation and would recommend it to anyone facing similar challenges. Study networks are applicable to a wide range of different courses. Both full-time and part-time students can benefit from them. We have learned that students are a resource in trying to improve the quality of their own experience; they are a major asset and one that can be very easily exploited. However these kinds of interventions need to be carefully planned. This 'student centred' approach has to have very clear objectives and explicit benefits. The design, the development and the planning take time and commitment but once a model emerges it can be refined and used again and again. We found the investment in the first year was higher, as it is with any new development, but reduced substantially on the second intake. One important lesson that emerged was that these kinds of innovations require a champion – someone who is committed and enthusiastic who will co-ordinate the scheme and involve other members of the team. The role of this individual needs to be widely recognised and resources allocated to fulfil that role.

A great deal of interest has been generated in the Business School by these developments. We have been approached by a number of Course Directors who are concerned about student support mechanisms. They see that study networks would be especially useful in supporting and motivating their students. The BA Business Studies part-time has experienced a number of benefits at a time when both staff and students are under pressure and we feel that these innovations are essential if we are to maintain the quality of the course and provide for an increase in student numbers.

Chapter 10

Thinking strategically: a subject group's attempts to maintain quality with reduced resources

Frank Webster

SUMMARY

The previous case studies have shown what individuals and course teams can achieve to hold on to quality. Subject groups and departments that co-operate to pool resources can achieve more than can isolated individuals but this requires academics to give up some of their autonomy concerning what and how they teach. This case study illustrates a broad-scale strategic approach implemented co-operatively. Here a sociology group decided to distinguish between courses which could be taught expensively and inexpensively. Expensive courses were those where much staff time was invested in preparation, classroom contact and assessment. These expensive courses could be run only by also designating other courses as cheap. These latter were usually lecture-based and assessed by unseen exams.

Background

One of the major features of higher education is the autonomy of staff. Appointed, as a rule, on the basis of achievement in individual research, many look to continue this in teaching specialist options; and yet each is also a member of a subject group which works together on programmes the aims and delivery of which can only be met by co-operation as a team.

In our context, teaching resources are provided in relation to the number of students who enrol on each module. In my subject group – and I doubt we are exceptional – half of total teaching resources come from teaching on just two large first-year single-term modules, so it is unavoidable that these are team taught. Moreover, while it is theoretically possible to trace resources to individuals using calculations of the number of students each teaches, we recognise that this is, at best, an approximation to real demands on staff, since it does not discriminate between pedagogic requirements or difficulty of topics.

Like it or not we work in a team. Our subject group is responsible for what, depending on student choice, is between one-third and two-thirds of an undergraduate degree programme. In this chapter I focus on ways in which this subject group has tried to think strategically about how to cope with increasingly large classes.

The driving force for that strategy, and for the policies that stem from it, has been a determination to ensure the maximum quality of teaching and learning possible commensurate with high quality academic content. But before I review the strategy it must be said that more students – without additional resources – were not of our choosing. Increased student numbers threaten to, and do in some cases, diminish the quality of what we offer. Coping with a rise in staff–student ratios (SSRs) in the discipline from 12:1 to 20:1 from 1981 to 1991 has been just that – a coping exercise. There have been improvements, as I shall make clear, but these have been in spite of cuts and decidedly not because of them.

I believe that another admission should also be made, one which is germane to the strategic response I shall review below. An increase in student numbers in excess of 60 per cent has meant that, whatever counter measures we may take, we are simply much busier than before. There are more things to do than previously. A major consequence of this has been unrelenting pressure on that which is most easily pushed aside in the short term ie research, scholarship, reading and all that which underwrites the knowledge base of academic life. If this knowledge base is not prioritised and protected, then all else is at risk. If staff lack time, energy, 'space' and motivation for high level academic work (ie research) then no matter how inspired the teaching or ingenious the course structure, the entire project is of dubious value.

But not all higher education is gloom and doom. Indeed, what is striking is that there have been some remarkable advances. In particular, there has been over the past decade and more:

- recognition that there are better ways of teaching than previously. One result is that pedagogy is more imaginative and interesting and that the teacher is now regarded as considerably more than a knowledgeable expert in his or her field;
- acknowledgement that there are other things to teach than the academic subject. I am thinking here of the range of transferable skills (communicative, analytical, information seeking, presentational, etc), of inestimable value to our students throughout their lives and careers;
- agreement that there are better ways of assessing student learning than the three-hour unseen examinations which once predominated in higher education: coursework, group activities, seminar performances, independent study etc.

I think that it is one of the finer achievements of higher education that we have made so much improvement in these areas by including them in the curriculum and consciously setting out to design degree programmes with them in mind. I believe also that, probably up to the mid-1980s, research and scholarship were strengthened in higher education. In all these areas it seems to me that a critical factor was the profile of the staff: young, enthusiastic, able and imaginative. Lecturers entering in the late sixties and early seventies had the interest, energy and openness to pioneer reform on many fronts. If we are to look anywhere to explain improvement in face of adversity it must be here, in the peculiarities of the staff profile.

Unfortunately those staff are now ageing, and with the grey hair and wrinkles, aggravated by continued reductions in resources, has come a mounting sense of malaise. There are unmistakable signs of a threshold having passed, and a downward path having been taken as regards research activity. Morale – somewhat volatile, but essential to the entire enterprise – appears to be low among colleagues, and still more students are being crammed into our institutions. There is real sense of ongoing crisis in higher education as we enter the nineties with no hope of an improvement in resources. How, in these circumstances, are we to do anything to maintain quality?

Thinking strategically

A key requirement is to stop acting in an ad hoc and piecemeal way, to stop responding to cuts in resources and the reality of ever more students on one's courses by 'making do'. Patching here and there while endeavouring to offer much the same as we did 15 years ago and trying to include improvements at the same time is simply untenable. Thinking strategically requires acting as a team to consider the overall aims of the programme, to reflect on what is achievable and at what costs, to prioritise areas of work on the degree, to consider and compare ideals and realities, and to decide how best one might go about attaining some goals with the minimum of negative consequences for others.

Getting a group of staff to think strategically is no mean achievement in itself. Academics are a notoriously independent breed of professionals used to working in their own way in realms where they alone are the specialist. They do not succumb readily to collective discipline. Furthermore, just surviving in face of mounting pressures takes much of one's energies and the last thing colleagues want is a series of lengthy meetings where one seeks to establish common goals and an agreed plan. In addition, any reader working in education will know the discord that can be caused by attempts to establish, say, research as a priority for a department, to be placed above 'open door' availability to students. Readers will probably also have experienced the difficulties that can be encountered in trying to persuade specialists in one aspect of the discipline to contribute to other parts of the course which the team thinks necessary.

After a lengthy series of meetings, in and out of the institution, my group did agree that decisive measures had to be taken to sustain the knowledge base of the staff. If we could not act successfully to ensure the quality of content – and we all thought that by the late 1980s it was endangered and that we could not continue to draw on resources built up in better times – then our courses were just not credible. If we could no longer offer state-of-the-art syllabuses, if, for instance, we were teaching labour relations with cases from the seventies, social policy which was not deeply informed about current debates and controversy, theory that could not engage with post-modernist and contemporary feminist thought, then this qualitative decline spelled the end.

Once this decision had been made it followed that something had to give in order to sustain research and scholarship. Candid discussion and considerable anguish led us, inexorably, to two particular areas in search of ways to reduce commitments – assessment and course delivery. Both of these were precious to us, and we had all invested much time and commitment to developing them, so we were extremely reluctant to let anything go, especially since we were convinced that we had made definite progress in areas that were now to be cut.

Assessment

Over the years assessment procedures – how we assess as well as what we assess – have changed quite radically. From the point of view of our students, and the educational venture in general, these have been changes for the good. The shift away from reliance on unseen examinations as the major quality discriminator, from requiring students to write four essays in three hours, with ten or a dozen papers spread over a fortnight in May, was long overdue.

The introduction of coursework, and its promotion from minority to often majority status, along with variations in what constituted coursework (essays, projects, dossiers, seminar papers, group presentations and so on), was more popular with our students, more appropriate for them (especially for the increased numbers of mature students), and tapped forms of learning which for far too long had been blocked, such as communication skills, and investigative abilities.

All of this was positive, but the major problem with coursework assessment, as every lecturer in higher education knows, is that it imposes a huge burden on the teacher. Marking, discussion, counselling, advising and debriefing are central features of coursework. This may have been sustainable at SSRs of 10:1, but when classes of over 100 in year one and often in excess of 40 at advanced level are typical, then teachers can find themselves constantly marking, on a treadmill of tutorials with students discussing aspects of their assessment and constantly rushing to fulfil rising student expectations.

It was noticeable at my institution that what had begun as a drift towards coursework in the late seventies and had established itself as the norm in the eighties on each course, was seriously silting up the system. Typically there would be a divide of something like 60 per cent examination and 40 per cent coursework on each option. In this situation, and under continuous resource depletion, some members of staff recalled the 'cost effectiveness' of the old order. There is nothing cheaper than a course assessed solely by an unseen examination – no problems of marking several pieces of work, of reporting back to the students, of co-ordinating a team of assessors who may have to account for a wide variety of coursework projects; nothing but 'Choose three questions from six to answer in three hours'. Of course, no one advocated a return to examinations because they were educationally discredited.

On the other hand, staff were being squeezed hard from pressure of having to mark a mountain of coursework and conduct tutorials with large numbers of students. It was becoming commonplace for staff to complain that they were 'giving' all the time, feeling academically drained and incapable of thinking freshly about their material.

The upshot was that the subject team felt compelled to analyse the undergraduate programme as a whole with an eye to reducing commitments. This revealed that almost everything we taught was by a 'mixed mode' of coursework and examination. Designing our options pretty much individually we had all adopted this convention. But looking at the course as a whole it was suggested that we could relieve the load on staff appreciably if, instead of leaving decisions about assessment to the individual lecturer (who moved, reasonably enough, with the trend towards coursework with examinations), we looked at the progress of students through the entire course and, if we could build into its structure mechanisms which ensured students could be exposed to a variety of modes of assessment, then perhaps we could justify reversion to some assessment by examination alone. Further, we could decide as a group to stop opting for 'mixed mode' assessment as a matter of routine, determining perhaps that certain options were best assessed by coursework while others could be quite effectively assessed by examinations.

This decision to develop a strategic policy towards assessment, one which ensured students would encounter several forms of assessment in their student days, required careful planning. We needed to look particularly at the assessment of compulsory aspects of the course to avoid students voting with their feet to avoid what they saw as 'unfriendly' examinations. Nonetheless it led colleagues to reconsider their assessment procedures and, in some cases, to look again at the virtues of examinations. Moreover, it led us to be more imaginative with examinations than we had been in the past: for example using various lengths of exam, seen and unseen exams and non-essay examinations. We are even considering multiple choice questions on one option.

In terms of one sort of quality I think this reversal to examinations signalled a significant retreat. Quality of assessment had advanced with the introduction of coursework and it was a retrograde step to halt it. But continual progress on the assessment front itself seriously threatened the quality of content. A return to examinations, in a carefully considered strategy which would preserve some of the gains made in assessment, was a consolidating factor. It allowed staff some much needed relief, some support for research which had to be boosted if quality content was to be maintained.

Course delivery

Changes in course delivery required still more radical surgery. Like most higher education institutions we taught our courses pretty much in a received mode: lectures, seminars, and tutorials characterised delivery in almost all of our work at the start of the eighties. Of course many colleges even calculated workloads in this way and each member of staff would teach a given number of hours in the form of lectures, seminars, and tutorials. If a 15–17 hours per week teaching load was not calculated, then teaching was estimated from SSRs which translated into contact with students of about the same hours.

The obvious problem with either version of this system was that it buckled under pressure from unrelenting rises in student numbers. Where staff worked on an hours basis, class size expanded alarmingly: seminar groups shot up to 14, 16, even as high as 20; tutorials from one or two to three or four. Where SSRs were the basis – and they rapidly became the norm because of their flexibility in accommodating additional student numbers – then tutorial loads in particular boosted teaching demands. At the end of the decade these pressures could no longer be contained, and the more students that arrived the more obvious this became. In our team the decisive decision, the one that released the building head of steam, was to separate the issue of resources and student numbers from that of course delivery. We decided to abandon the practice of each member of staff being responsible for generating a certain unit of resource (ie being responsible for a given number of students) and then presuming that each member, delivering his or her options in a similar way, would carry the same teaching load.

As a group we decided that we would not be able to maintain the quality of content we desired unless we moved to reduce contact with students. Having made up our minds about this, but still wishing to retain at least some of the ways of teaching which we knew were valuable, we planned to structure the course in terms of 'cheap' and 'expensive' forms of delivery. By 'cheap' we meant, above all, economical in terms of staff time. Hence

	'Expensive' Module	'Cheap' Module
Enrolment	300 students	160 students
Student contact time	1 hr lecture/week 1 hrs seminar/week 1 hr individual tutorial/term	2 hrs lectures/week 1 hr seminar/week
Staff contact time per week	1 hr lecture 20 hrs seminars 30 hrs tutorials Total: 51 hrs/week Total for term: 510 hrs	2 hrs lectures 12 hrs seminars 4 'office hours' Total: 22 hrs/week Total for term: 220 hrs
Assessment tasks	Seminar presentation (20%) Seminar paper (20%) Essay (50%) Library work (10%)	2 hr unseen examination (100%)
Marking time	45 hrs/week Total: 450 hrs	None during term 40 hrs for exam Total: 40 hrs
Total staff time:	960 hrs	260 hrs
Staff hrs/student:	3.20 hrs	1.63 hrs

Table 10.1 Costings of 'expensive' and 'cheap' first-year modules

these modules would be organised around lectures and seminars which would concentrate on clarifying points arising in these and from independent student reading. There would be no tutorial support, a limited number of 'office hours' would be available to students on a 'waiting room' or 'surgery' basis, and assessment would be entirely by examinations. Conversely, 'expensive' modules were ones which called for a lot of staff input. This revolved around seminar work and required extensive support from prepared teaching materials, lengthy tutorial work with individual students, and use of a variety of coursework assignments for assessment which needed considerable feedback to, and discussion with, students.

A better idea of the distinction between 'cheap' and 'expensive' modules, and some idea of the magnitude of resource differences, can be gained from Tables 10.1 and 10.2, describing examples of first-year and second/third-year modules. The calculations make clear that our 'cheap' modules are between one-half and one-third of the cost of our 'expensive' ones. To be sure, neither of the tables take into account preparation time, the hidden mass of all teaching, and it should be noted that the 'expensive' modules are exceptionally demanding in this respect since they require so much prepared teaching material for students.

Central to this strategy was organisation of the course as a whole to ensure that as the individual student moved through the system she or he

	'Expensive' Module	'Cheap' Module
Enrolment	45 students	60 students
Student contact time	1 hr lecture/week 2 hrs seminar/week 1 hr individual tutorial/term	2 hrs lectures/week
Staff contact time per week	1 hr lecture 6 hrs seminars 4.5 hrs tutorials Total: 11.5 hrs/week Total for term: 115 hrs	2 hrs lectures 4 'office hours' Total: 6 hrs/week Total for term: 60 hrs
Assessment tasks	Seminar presentation (20%) Seminar contribution (10%) Seminar paper (20%) Essay (50%)	2 hr unseen examination (100%) (3 essay questions from 6)
Marking time	6 hrs/week Total: 60 hrs	None during term 15 hrs for exam Total: 15 hrs
Total staff time:	175 hrs	75 hrs
Staff hrs/student:	3.89 hrs	1.25 hrs

Table 10.2 Costings of 'expensive' and 'cheap' second- and third-year modules

would encounter various types of course delivery. We guaranteed this by redesigning compulsory parts of the course to ensure that some elements were 'cheap' and others 'expensive'.

Further, we opted not to take the route of teaching all of the first-year modules 'cheap' in order to pay for second and third years' advanced and 'expensive' work. We were agreed that first-year students should not be used as fodder. Indeed, we determined to teach the introductory course (a class of some 300 students) in an intensive manner for two reasons. The first was that it is when they first arrive in higher education institutions that students most need close personal attention: to give them some reassurance, to provide detailed feedback on standards and to introduce oneself. The second was so we could teach them effectively how we expected them to cope with the course as a whole, particularly as they encountered a 'cheap' course in their second term.

To this end, we revolved the introductory course around seminars and one-to-one tutorials with a detailed and lengthy workbook (383 pages) providing a guide and text for much of their later study. In the seminars and tutorials students were encouraged to take responsibility for their own learning, instructed in how to find information effectively, given clear guidance about how to produce written work in an academic milieu and so forth.

We felt that teaching this in an intensive way, whatever the demands on staff, was especially useful early in the students' days at the Polytechnic. That way we could maximise the effectiveness of learning during their time here: if we set them off on the right road about how to conduct a seminar effectively (something which requires detailed debriefing after the session and considerable advice before it is undertaken), then they could get off to a fast start in developing essential transferable skills.

Teaching 'cheap' does not mean teaching badly. Where lectures become central to a course, then they must be imaginatively conducted, supported by precise guides and reading lists, they should be interesting and engaging, and where students are getting but one seminar per week these must be planned thoroughly and students given sound advice on how to get most benefit from them.

Problems

It has to be conceded that a policy of cross-subsidisation is fraught with problems, several of which will have already struck the reader. Let me signal just four of them:

1. A requisite is a co-operative and well-knit group of staff. Since resources have been separated from course delivery in the sense that the teaching hours available for a module are no longer considered to follow automatically from the number of students enrolling on the module, members of the team must be willing to forgo a narrow view of their commitments. If one member were to insist that since option x – however it may be taught – generates numbers of students y and hence requires teaching resources z, then the entire strategy is undermined. It is essential that reasons for the group to support 'expensive' ways of teaching are discussed and agreed by all. This is a particularly fraught matter when it comes to introducing new members of staff to the group. Understandably they are wary and suspicious: eager to know their precise commitments, they may take considerable persuasion that they are being treated fairly.

2. Similarly, though we do cross-subsidise, we have found it extremely difficult to quantify this in a satisfactory manner. How does one allocate appropriate resources to a module designer who may only teach a small part of the module? How does one regard responsibility for lectures as opposed to the seminars on a module? How much resource does workbook preparation merit as opposed to seminar leadership? Short of producing complex and time-consuming formulae, it has to be acknowledged that one's workload cannot be reduced to the resource generated by the number of students. In these circumstances one must then proceed by a sense of judgement and feel for equity. Doubtless some figures could be put on all of this, but for the while we proceed on the

basis of goodwill and trust among mutually supportive colleagues. I am not at all sure that this can be guaranteed in the long term.

3. Faced with continued reductions in the resource which comes with each student it is becoming increasingly difficult to sustain 'expensive' teaching, especially on large introductory courses. Given the shift in higher education to an American model, then it may be that all first-year work should be taught cheap in order to support advanced classes and the required research base amongst staff.

4. In my institution modules are routinely evaluated by students. Returns over the years reveal a very clear pattern of hostility towards unseen examinations and preferences for increased coursework assessment. There is student pressure towards increasing workloads on staff. Teachers can make some reasoned responses to those calls not least by emphasising the trend in examination results which appears to indicate no significant difference in outcomes between forms of assessment. Nonetheless, this is a defensive action which will not end the student dissatisfaction. Against this, evaluations have suggested that, from the perspective of the individual student, the very different pressures imposed on staff by the form of course delivery is not fully appreciated. After all, to the student a single tutorial is not very much over the course of a term (and a good number can get some limited access in office hours) and the seminars, though different in form, still occupy the same amount of time for them.

Conclusion

Quite simply, for those of us in higher education to go on as if continual cuts can be accommodated in the established manner is unsustainable, particularly if one wishes to incorporate pedagogic and assessment reforms. To cope in the present climate, strategic thinking is essential. This chapter has focussed on two consequences of that sort of thinking in one team of lecturers. My view is that the measures taken retain important elements of quality in teaching and assessment (which are unavoidably less than ideal), simultaneous with giving staff some space to protect the most important dimension of their work – the quality of their knowledge.

Chapter 11

Teaching large classes: the institutional perspective

Clive Booth and David Watson

SUMMARY

Some of the innovations recorded in the case studies could be replicated by individuals and course teams elsewhere. However, in some cases individuals would find that their institutional culture and practices would block these changes.

For innovation to be widespread requires strong institutional support. For example, Ashley Green's account of a radically redesigned physics course (Chapter Seven) was supported by a number of institutional features, including participation in a year-long, part-time course in teaching methods for new teaching staff, an educational consultant on course design, a well resourced print room, funding for staff to redesign courses, a central computer software system which enabled rapid marking of objective tests and comprehensive course evaluation and no institutional requirement as to the number of contact hours he was required to teach. To varying extents the other case studies from Oxford Polytechnic have been aided by these and other institutional initiatives. Without strong top-level institutional support little can be achieved.

In this chapter Clive Booth, Director of Oxford Polytechnic and David Watson, Director of Brighton Polytechnic, set out how heads of institutions and key committees can aid staff in innovating to cope with larger classes.

Funding context

For most of this century the single model of British higher education, consisting of lectures and tutorials delivered to small groups of students, has gone unchallenged. Even after the Conservative and Labour governments of the early 1960s committed themselves to a massive expansion of the system, it took some time for the implications of wider participation to emerge in public debate; and even then interest focussed much more on the question whether a larger proportion of 18 year-olds were capable of benefiting, than on the ways in which the delivery of higher education might have to change.

Concerned about the public expenditure implications of expansion, Shirley Williams, then a junior minister in the Department of Education and Science (DES), proposed in 1968 a long list of ways in which the 'productivity' of higher education could be increased. The proposals included increasing student–staff ratios from around 7:1 to perhaps 10:1 or 11:1; encouraging more students to study within reach of home; securing the more efficient use of buildings and equipment; avoiding duplication of facilities; encouraging sharing between universities and polytechnics of various services; changes in the system of student support, including the possibilities of loans; new ways of organising the academic year; and the expansion of distance learning. Her initiative received a genteel rebuff from the Committee of Vice Chancellors and Principals and it is a measure of the non-interventionist stance of central government at the time that her suggestions were not pursued more forcefully.

The creation of the polytechnics in 1969–71 introduced a new institutional form into higher education, based on the tradition of further education colleges run by local government. The polytechnics did not inherit the university tradition of collegiality and self-government: their organisation was more hierarchical and it was not accidental that their chief officers were usually given the title 'director'. This emphasis on management as opposed to participative self-government was to have important consequences for the development of the polytechnics and their approach to expansion, resourcing and teaching and learning.

By the end of the 1970s the polytechnics had grown to the point where many of them enrolled more undergraduate students than the average university. The 1970s were a time of plenty for institutions' revenue or recurrent budgets. (Capital, including capital building was another story as institutions struggled with a parsimonious DES and local authorities trapped in the absurdity of devising and completing capital plans on a one-year cycle.) However, for general expenditure, 'pooling' – the system of funding which enabled institutions to spend public money on a scale limited mainly by the self-restraint of the local authorities which maintained them – was the engine of growth. It was abruptly ended soon after the change of government in 1979 and replaced by a 'capped' pool, by which the total sum available for the local authority-maintained polytechnics and colleges was fixed in advance. The new organisation set up to allocate funds, the National Advisory Body (NAB), adopted an ingenious formula by which the best route to institutional salvation lay through the most rapid possible growth in enrolments regardless of the funds available. The effect on the resources available per student (the 'unit of resource') can be seen in Table 11.1.

Efforts by some polytechnics and colleges to marshal collective resistance to the funding regime were frustrated by a failure to find common ground: many of those dedicated to increasing participation in higher education felt that this could only be achieved by permitting the unit of resource to fall and that this would not necessarily mean a fall in academic standards. By contrast, the universities and their funding body, the University Grants Committee, shared the view that the traditional university education

Table 11.1 Higher education: unit public funding

real terms index (1981-82 = 100)

Financial Years	1981-82 actual	1982-83 actual	1983-84 actual	1984-85 actual	1985-86 actual	1986-87 actual	1987-88 actual	1988-89 actual
Universities (GB)[1]	100	103	104	103	101	100	99	100
Polytechnics and colleges (England)[2]	100	96	91	88	85	87	83	81

Source: Public Expenditure White Paper, 1991, p. 23

1: The index for universities is derived from a division of total UGC/UFC recurrent grant and tuition fee income for home and EC students by the financial year average of relevant full-time equivalent student numbers.

2: The index for polytechnics and colleges is derived from a division of their aggregate expenditure (gross of tuition fees but excluding miscellaneous income) by financial year full-time equivalent student numbers.

required a level of unit funding that could not be reduced without lowering standards and, as the table shows, they were successful in maintaining the real value of the unit of resource through the 1980s.

With the creation in 1989 of independent polytechnics and colleges and a new funding council, the Polytechnic and Colleges Funding Council (PCFC), came increased competitive pressure. The PCFC required institutions to submit priced bids for 'contracts' to provide student places and the early results of bidding indicate that the squeeze begun by NAB has been successfully maintained.

Meanwhile, the UGC's successor, the Universities Funding Council (UFC), attempted to introduce a mildly competitive bidding system which was abandoned when most universities followed the guide prices suggested by the Council. Speculation now centres on the policies likely to be adopted by the unified funding councils (one each for England, Scotland and Wales) which will succeed the PCFC and UFC, but it would be surprising if the pressures on institutions to provide for more students at lower unit costs did not continue. In practical terms this will probably mean pressure on universities to achieve something approaching the 'efficiency gain' demonstrated by the PCFC sector over the past decade.

What are the implications of these financial pressures for the delivery of higher education? Perhaps most importantly, they have forced many institutions and teachers to change their focus from formal teaching towards support for student learning and to reconsider the ways in which the time of the teacher can be best used to promote learning. Institutional managers have similarly been concerned to move away from the historic preoccupation with the resources devoted to formal teaching and the past obsession with 'contact time'. Some of the accompanying changes, such as the negotiation of a new contract for teachers in the PCFC sector, have been painful. Different patterns of resource distribution between teaching, library, computing, reprographics and other support services need also to be considered as students become increasingly reliant on out-of-classroom facilities. Students are entitled to know what they can expect of the institution in terms of the support it will provide them with.

Institutional responses

Institutional heads have to tread a fine line between resisting over-rapid change (for example, by arguing the case for realistic funding with government) and appearing to be unconcerned about the academic and quality-of-life implications of diminishing resources. This underlines the importance of developing institutional strategies for coping with change and especially providing mechanisms that enable staff to adapt. Part of this process must be directed at ensuring that the reasons for change are shared and understood by staff at all levels. This in itself is a daunting challenge in a large institution and will require groups of influential people, such as heads of department or course leaders, to be actively involved in developing and promulgating the strategy. Half-day workshops for such staff are one means of helping them to come to grips with the issues and preparing them for their own role in promoting change.

At Oxford Polytechnic, the Educational Methods Unit (EMU) and Modular Course organisation have both produced programmes on themes related to coping with large classes. Under the Staff Release Scheme administered by EMU, individual teachers can apply for modest funding to relieve them of part of their regular teaching duties in order to develop learning support materials (See Appendix 11-A). EMU also organises lunch-time seminars which encourage the sharing of common problems and good practice. The Modular Course, which covers more than two-thirds of the Polytechnic's undergraduate teaching, initiates research and evaluation projects and seminars designed to examine the implications of new patterns of teaching and learning.

One important advantage of this arrangement is that it bridges the departmental and faculty structures, bringing together different cultures and disciplines to share best practice. A parallel set of initiatives has focussed on heads of department encouraging them to review contact time norms for particular subjects, to scrutinise carefully the amount of staff time spent in generating and completing assessment, and look at means of student support other than traditional lectures and seminars (such as timetabled 'office hours', 'surgeries' and 'drop-in' sessions).

Such central initiatives need to be accompanied by systematic discussion at the level of course teams as part of the normal cycle of reviewing and redesigning courses or modules. At Oxford the annual review process is used to ask course teams to give special consideration to particular problems. Recent examples include literacy, approaches to student feedback and assessment strategies. However, it is important that senior management should have confidence in the teams' ability to devise solutions that support their own students' needs.

With the increasing devolution of financial responsibility to departments, ways need to be found of encouraging the staff development policies adopted by each department to give adequate attention to teaching and learning alongside the research interests and the personal growth of staff. At Oxford, the development of individual departmental statements which feed into the strategic plan provide one means of calling departments to account. The new staff appraisal system being introduced in 1991-2 will encourage individual staff members to review how their teaching methods can be improved.

Physical space for teaching and learning is a more intractable problem at Oxford as in many other polytechnics. Buildings designed 20 or more years ago do not offer the right distribution of types and sizes of room needed today. Very large lecture theatres, rooms for independent working, computer terminal rooms: these are examples of the sorts of space that are in short supply. Timetabling problems are exacerbated by the pressures of greatly increased numbers. Initiatives such as extending the teaching timetable into the evenings, the weekends and traditional vacation times can help but do not fully solve the problem of inappropriately configured or poorly maintained buildings. Without substantial increases in funding for new or adapted buildings it is hard to see what institutions can do, except make the best of what they have.

Management obligations

The primary responsibility for institutional managers seeking to bring about the changes imposed by the funding context with the least possible damage to teaching and learning has to be to maintain good systems of communication. It is important that staff responsible for implementing change at the course level understand institutional constraints, share institutional goals, and remain committed to the preservation of the highest possible standards within the resources available. Appreciating the wider context also assists in avoiding the morale trap which occurs when individual teachers have to change practices which they see as central to their academic traditions. Adopting a clear, public, cross-institutional set of policies in learning support is reassuring for the individual who might otherwise feel that he or she is 'letting go' or 'letting the side down'.

Equally important is resistance to specious arguments about constraint, alone leading to improvements in quality. The history of educational innovation refutes the thesis that the way to achieve positive change is to *reduce* the resources available. While maintaining the case for matching the expansion of the higher education system with new resources externally, the institutional manager must stress the obligations assumed on behalf of the students admitted to the college and work with other staff to maximise the quality of the student experience.

Some specific strategies (including those mentioned above) are helpful here. Together they should be directed at making space for innovation; for example by anticipating (and not merely following) the continued decline of the unit of resource per student in order to create resources for staff development. It is also important to maintain the dialogue about the effective division of resources between traditional teaching inputs and other aspects of learning resources, and to discourage fixation on inappropriate performance indicators (such as 'class hours', still collected by the DES, and for certain purposes the student–staff ratio).

We have set out our suggestions for a planned institutional response to teaching large classes in summary form in Appendix 11-B. Not all of them will be appropriate to every institution but institutional leaders and managers ought at least to ensure that they are systematically considered. The process of debate will help to raise awareness of the institutional concern for coming to grips with the challenge of large classes.

Conclusion

Not many staff in British higher education would have forecast ten years ago the enormous changes that have taken place since then. The DES itself produced a consultative paper (*Higher Education in the 1990s*) predicting a contraction of the system instead of the burgeoning demand for places that has been the reality! Few would have been bold enough to predict that the increase in 'efficiency' represented by the 20 per cent rise in the ratio of students to staff could have been achieved without an obvious fall in standards of student achievement. Yet the reports of HMI, professional bodies and external examiners suggest that standards have been maintained and in some cases have risen. That this has been possible is a tribute to both staff and students. If our prediction of a continuing squeeze on resources is correct, it will call for a greater commitment from institutions to support the continuing evolution of new methods of teaching and learning. This will be especially true of some universities for whom the process has scarcely begun.

Appendix 11-A

Enabling change: a staff release scheme

Central idea

Staff faced with increased student numbers need 'time out' to consider new ways of teaching. Otherwise increased student numbers mean staff have less opportunity to develop coherent strategies.

Basic features

A sum of money is top sliced from the institutional budget (at Oxford Polytechnic in 1992–3 it is £20,000). Staff bid competitively for funds to support proposed projects. The money can be used to hire in part-time staff so enabling project staff to plan and implement change and/or to pay for secretarial and technician time to produce materials.

A group of teaching staff consider bids in terms of stated criteria. At Oxford Polytechnic in 1992–3 these included:

- Priority will be given to projects concerned with coping with large classes and high SSRs.
- It should be clear from the proposals what the likely total impact will be. Both the extent of the educational impact (ie in terms of numbers of students, number of student-hours) and the significance of likely impact (ie how dramatic to the individuals concerned) should be made clear.
- It should be clear from the proposals what the likely total impact of the project on other staff will be, and what knock-on effects in terms of teaching on other modules by other staff there are likely to be.
- Projects which have clear trans-polytechnic relevance will be considered favourably.

Examples of staff release projects: Oxford Polytechnic 1990–1

Department	Funding	Description of Project
Engineering	£1000	Selection of OU Physics materials to create individual-study based modules.
Social Studies	£785	Revision of Sociology workbook incorporating and developing enterprise skills content.

Department	Funding	Description of Project
Business	£600	Developing a Macroeconomics workbook, incorporating enterprise skills.
Geography	£800	Development of student-directed writing syndicates as a means to improving students' writing and collaborative skills.
Computing, Mathematics & Statistics	£2630	Generation of self-paced teaching material for computer mapping package.
Computing, Mathematics & Statistics	£1300	Developing a software engineering case study that covers all the stages of software development.
Social Studies	£1500	Developing a workbook and producing linked audio and video tapes for new evening module Ethnicity and Health.
Education	£2350	Team development of a learning package incorporating self-assessment and profiling for MEd.
Languages	£850	Development of computer-assisted language learning material for German.
Geology	£600	Development of a self-teaching package for Introduction to Geology.
Business	£800	Continuation of the development of a database for the teaching aids and materials in the Accounting Resource Centre.

Appendix 11-B

A planned institutional response to teaching large classes

1. Promoting innovation

a) Promote a culture of innovation. Let everyone know that innovation is expected and will be supported.

b) Show a realistic concern for the problems facing lecturers in making change. Beware orders from on high to implement sweeping changes in unrealistically short timescales without consultation.

c) Develop course monitoring and review procedures which foster rather than block innovation and diversity.

d) Give the maximum local discretion to course teams to decide how to deliver courses: avoid a single institutional model.

e) Consider the advantages of modularisation. Oxford's experience of modularisation has been that, because it transcends departmental boundaries, it stimulates change both in curriculum and teaching method.

2. Incentives and rewards

f) Build in incentives to greater efficiency. Make sure that resources follow students and that staff can see a connection between increased teaching efficiency and more time for research and professional development.

g) Raise the status of teaching by promotion opportunities specifically for teaching achievement.

3. Support services

h) Provide a wide range of efficient technical back-up services (eg desktop publishing for workbooks, automated multiple choice marking) which are top sliced rather than recharged to departments.

i) Support a central focus for innovation and staff development and training, such as an Education Methods Unit (see text), to disseminate best practice through seminar programmes, a teaching newsletter and a resource centre. Provide training in techniques for large-group lecturing.

4. Funding Schemes

j) Fund a staff release scheme. The Oxford scheme (Appendix 11-A) provides very modest but effective funds to enable staff to develop teaching materials and study good practice elsewhere.

k) Fund evaluation studies undertaken by staff themselves as a means of encouraging debate about successful practice.

5. Accommodation and facilities

l) Increase the efficient use of space by central timetabling of accommodation and minor works to enable rooms to be used more effectively.

m) Ensure that such centrally timetabled accommodation is well-maintained and equipped with audio visual aids.

n) Provide more private study space, especially in libraries.

o) Invest in information technology, with 24 hour access computer rooms and terminal points in halls of residence as well as throughout teaching buildings.

6. Implementation and accountability

p) Hold specific senior members of staff, not just committees, accountable for preparing an implementation plan for the above ideas and carrying it through.

Chapter 12

Conclusion: improving teaching and learning in large classes

Graham Gibbs and Alan Jenkins

SUMMARY

As well as learning about the case studies described in the preceding chapters, we have worked with lecturers in many institutions who are faced with rapid increases in student numbers and who need to redesign their courses to cope. We have seen innovations both succeed and fail and have seen courses declining in quality where no changes have been made. From our experiences we have tried to pull together some general guidelines for the consideration of anyone teaching larger classes with reduced resources and who cares about quality.

Courses and resources

Cost your course

It is often a revelation to lecturers to discover what their courses cost in terms of teaching hours, and what aspects of their courses generate the bulk of these costs. The kinds of analysis illustrated in the case studies may reveal that assessment uses up twice as many teaching hours as teaching (Table 7.1), or that while for one way of delivering a course the costs increase in proportion to the number of students, a different design becomes increasingly economic as student numbers increase. It is difficult to make rational and effective decisions about how to cope with reduced resources if you have no clear idea how resources are spent at the moment or what the resource implications of alternatives might be.

Table 12.1, an example of an Education course for 72 students, provides a useful framework for costing as it identifies teaching and assessment costs per student. It can be seen that the new course involves only 36 per cent of the original teaching costs per student (ie 1 as opposed to 2.75 hours per

Original Course	Staff Time	Staff Time	New Course
Teaching			
Lectures (18 weeks x 2 hrs)	36 hrs	36 hrs	Workshops (18 weeks x 2 hrs)
Seminars (18 weeks x 9 groups of 8)	162 hrs	36 hrs	Autonomous seminars (18 weeks x 2 tutors touring 6 groups of 12)
Total teaching hours	198 hrs	72 hrs	
Total teaching hours/student	2.75 hrs	1.00 hrs	
Assessment			
Essays (72 x 2 essays at 20 mins)	48 hrs	6 hr	Multiple choice question tests (6 x 1 hrs administration)
Examination (72 x 2 questions at 10 mins)	24 hrs	18 hrs	
		36 hrs	Seminar presentations (Peer assessed, 1hr/week collation) Portfolio (72 at 30 mins)

Table 12.1 An example of an education course for 72 students

student). You should be able to undertake a similar analysis of your own course and its possible alternatives.

Vary your methods

There is an extraordinary uniformity of course design and delivery in many parts of higher education in the UK despite a wide variety of course aims. However some types of course (for example those involving well specified and documented knowledge and procedures) can be effectively taught relatively cheaply while others may be very difficult to teach without extensive staff and other resources. Common approaches to coping with large classes are unlikely to be appropriate across a whole degree programme. Efficient and effective designs will vary investments, teaching some parts at a fraction of the cost of other parts (for example see Frank Webster's discussion of resource-rich and resource-poor courses in Chapter Ten). Even where there are existing variations in resourcing, there may be alternatives. For example, first-year courses are often taught more cheaply than third-year courses, but it might be more effective to develop students' independence early on and then teach more advanced courses more economically.

Different course objectives will require different methods with different resource implications. Uniformity of course delivery is often a sign of both ineffective and inefficient course design.

Don't exhaust all your resources on teaching staff

Coping with large classes involves different teaching and learning accommodation, more learning resources such as books, printed materials and IT, support staff and special technical support services. The overall balance between teaching staff and other resources will need to be different if relatively expensive teaching staff are to be employed to maximum effect. Some very large courses employ their own administrator simply to handle students' assignments, handouts and all other communications with students. This can take a huge burden off of lecturers, but requires a deliberate decision to move some resources away from teaching staff.

Clarify your objectives

It is difficult to decide what to cut and what to save if there are no clear objectives for a course. It is important to be realistic about what can be achieved with the students and resources (and energy) you have, rather than try to hold on to what may always have been utopian ideals. This realism may well involve quite explicitly giving up some objectives in order to concentrate on the really important ones: better to achieve your main objectives than to miss them all. This may mean making tough decisions concerning the relative value of breadth or depth, content A or content B, content or skills, reducing failure or fostering excellence.

Student participation

Develop students' independence

If students are to learn more independently of tutors then they need to learn how to be independent. Some course structures can leave students dependent on being taught. Heavily taught students may never develop independence. It can be cost effective and educationally desirable to invest in efforts to develop students' independent learning skills, and their autonomy, as early in their courses as possible.

Get students to help themselves

Students can teach each other, give seminars in groups without tutors, comment and mark each other's work, design each other's experiments, supervise themselves, and undertake most of a tutor's roles. They may do it at a less sophisticated and reliable level, but what it loses in academic rigour it may gain in impact. Learning to undertake these tasks and roles is a profoundly educational process. As traditional models of tutoring become harder to resource many aspects can be replaced by student self- and peer-tutoring.

Treat contact with students as 'quality time'

Whether lectures or small group tutorials, treat your contact with students as precious time. Ration it, plan and prepare for it, organise your students to prepare for it, and get students to follow it up effectively. If there is to be less contact then it needs to be used purposefully rather than casually.

Don't provide all your support mechanisms for every student

Not all students need or even welcome extensive support. Some very able or independent students hardly need teachers at all, while others need frequent support 'on demand'. As it will not be possible to provide high levels of support for all students, design courses to provide a range of levels of support so that students use only that level of support which they need.

Communicate student objectives clearly

Students can learn independently suprisingly well if they understand where they are supposed to be going and what is on offer to help them to get there. Be explicit about objectives, assessment requirements and criteria, time-tables, topics and resources. Any ambiguity or disorganisation in the system will use up staff time coping with student confusion.

The process of change

Start changing now; make progress however you can

The funding situation is getting worse at an accelerating rate. The longer you delay radical change, the harder pressed you will be when radical change is pressed upon you by force of cicumstances. Some changes you will be able to make on your own, without permission or co-operation with others, for immediate implementation. Some things will require co-operation and a medium term perspective. Some changes involve institutional funding, permission from slow-moving bureaucracy or even external approval. Plan how different levels of change could be brought about. The important thing is to get moving as soon as possible.

Learn from experience

It is impossible to get everything right first time when you change a course. Notice what works and try to discover why. Where problems occur it may be quite minor mistakes which are to blame rather than the whole method or philosophy. Treat the process of course change as an ongoing experiment.

There are no recipes

We hope that the wide range of methods illustrated in the case studies demonstrate that there are no simple answers when deciding how to cope with more students. Effective change usually involves a collection of techniques used together in a unique way which suits the context.

Evaluate thoroughly

The costs involved in delivering large courses can be enormous and the costs or savings associated with different decisions about how to deliver large courses can also be substantial. It is therefore worth putting considerable effort into determining whether the key design decisions were correct by undertaking careful evaluations. Do students really put in the neccessary study hours if there is less class contact? Do the learning packages really lead students off into wider reading, or do they restrict what students read? These are questions for evaluation to answer. If you are being radical you may well encounter opposition and positive evaluation evidence can protect you. If you need extra resources to extend innovations, positive evaluations may win you those resources. Get good data to back your hunches.

Change is expensive

Rewriting lectures and updating conventional courses has always been seen as a normal part of an academic's job. Even revisions of degree programmes, for example for validation purposes, are not normally seen as imposing a burden over and above what would be expected. But the scale of some of the changes neccessary to cope with large classes does impose additional demands. Producing materials to suport a resource-based course obviously takes a great deal of writing time. But any new technique will take time to learn. The first lectures you gave probably took many days to write whereas you can now put a good lecture together in a fraction of the time. It is the same with any teaching method. The first few occasions take a great deal of time and effort in preparation and engender a good deal of anxiety. The staff development and preparation time neccessary first time round should not be underestimated. Substantial change is expensive and requires special additional funding – for example in the form of the staff release scheme described in Chapter Eleven. Without such funding, change is likely to be piecemeal or may fail through lack of investment.

Students need to learn how to change, too

Many of the case studies described above require students to spend their time in different ways and undertake different kinds of learning tasks. They may resist this change if they don't get any help in adjusting. The innovation may fail not because the lecturers don't know how to implement it, but because the *students* don't know how to implement it. Explain what you are doing and why. Explain the implications for their patterns of study. Be explicit about your expectations, your assignment requirements and your assessment criteria. Run study skill exercises if necessary. Give students the opportunity to talk about how they are managing on the course. They need to learn from their experience of learning on large courses.

These changes are not easy to implement. They require individuals, subject groups, institutions and national organisations (including government) to critically reappraise current practice and implement radical changes. However, without such changes staff will exhaust themselves trying to keep the traditional system going and the quality of student learning and the quality of the student experience will rapidly decline. We believe that the methods of course delivery described in this book can enable mass higher education systems to attain something that students and staff can recognise as quality. We wish you good luck in implementing those you consider useful and in devising other methods that better suit your students' needs.

Selective annotated bibliography

Andresen, L. W., (1988) *Lecturing to Large Groups: A Guide to Doing it Less But Better*, 2nd edn. Sydney, Professional Development Centre, University of New South Wales. Also available from SCED Publications, Learning Methods Unit, Birmingham Polytechnic, Perry Barr, Birmingham, B42 2SU.

Invaluable compendium of edited/abbreviated versions of previously published accounts of strategies used by lecturers to teach large student groups.

Andresen, L., Nightingale, P., Boud, D. and Magin, D., (1989) *Strategies for Assessing Students*. Sydney, Professional Development Centre, University of New South Wales. Also available from SCED Publications, Learning Methods Unit, Birmingham Polytechnic.

Suggests broad strategies for reappraising assessment methods, eg avoid over grading student work, and provides brief accounts of various methods that develop these strategies.

Benjamin, L. T., Daniel, R. S., and Brewer, C.L., (1985) *Handbook for Teaching Introductory Psychology*. New Jersey, Lawrence Erlbaum.

Reprints of articles from the journal Teaching Psychology *that are of value to those teaching large introductory psychology courses. The basic ideas, eg the use of computer marked examinations, are transferable to other disciplines.*

Coleman, H., (1989) *Learning and Teaching in Large Classes: a Bibliography*. Overseas Education Unit, Leeds University, Dept of Linguistics and Modern English, Lancaster University.

Mainly covers literature concerned with teaching English as a foreign language in large classes . It also partly considers the wider literature on large classes. Part of a project on teaching English as a foreign language to large classes, particularly in Third World countries.

Cryer, P. and Elton E., (1992) *Promoting Active Learning in Large Classes*. Sheffield, Universities Staff Development Unit.

A general intoduction to the issues and brief consideration of strategies in large lectures, seminars and laboratories.

Gibbs, G. (1992) *Lecturing to More Students; Assessing More Students; Problems & Course Design Strategies; Discussion with More Students; Independent Learning with More Students*. Oxford, Oxford Centre for Staff Development.

Five booklets which offer brief examples of strategies that can be adapted by teachers in any discipline. The booklets were designed to support workshops on these themes.

Gibbs G., Habeshaw S. and Habeshaw, T., (1992) *53 Interesting Ways to Teach Large Classes*. Bristol, Technical and Education Services.

A compendium of brief practical suggestions on most aspects of teaching large classes (lecturing, discussion, assessment) that can readily be adopted by teachers in all disciplines.

Magin, D., Nightingale, P., Andresen, L., and Boud, D. (1989) *Strategies for Increasing Students' Independence*. Sydney, Professional Development Centre, University of New South Wales. Also available from SCED Publications, Learning Methods Unit, Birmingham Polytechnic.

Suggests ways in which one can help students to be more independent of the teacher while probably reducing staff (contact) time. Provides brief summaries of a wide range of published sources.

McGee, R., (1986) (2nd edn 1991) *Teaching The Mass Class*. Washington, American Sociological Association.

Though directed at sociology classes of 250 plus, its ideas and suggestions are broadly applicable to other disciplines. Considers the problems of teaching large classes, organising and administering the mass class and doing mass class teaching. Written very much from and to the immediate experience of teaching mass classes.

McGee, R., (1991) *Handling Hordes; Teaching Large Classes*. West Lafayette, Ind, Continuing Education Office, Purdue University.

An educational video of a lecture/workshop by Reece McGee on how to handle the mass class. Includes sections on preparing for and organising the mass class, handling problem students, discipline and overcoming stage fright.

Weimer, M. G., (1987) *Teaching Large Classes Well*. San Francisco, Jossey Bass.

A variety of authors offer suggestions on aspects of mass class teaching including dealing with details in a large class, lecturing, essential communication strategies, and acquiring student feedback that improves instruction.

Index